BULLY

FOREVER WOLVES

First published in Great Britain by
Steve Bull Publishing

ISBN-978-0-9955634-0-7

Written by
Paul Berry and Tim Spiers

Designed by Simon Pagett
Synaxis Design Consultancy Limited
Molineux Stadium, Wolverhampton WV1 4QR

Printed and bound in the UK by
John Price Printers Limited
Brook Street, Bilston, West Midlands WV14 0NW

Photography courtesy of
Express and Star, AMA Sports Photography, PA Images, Sam Bagnall, Dave Bagnall, Ed Bagnall

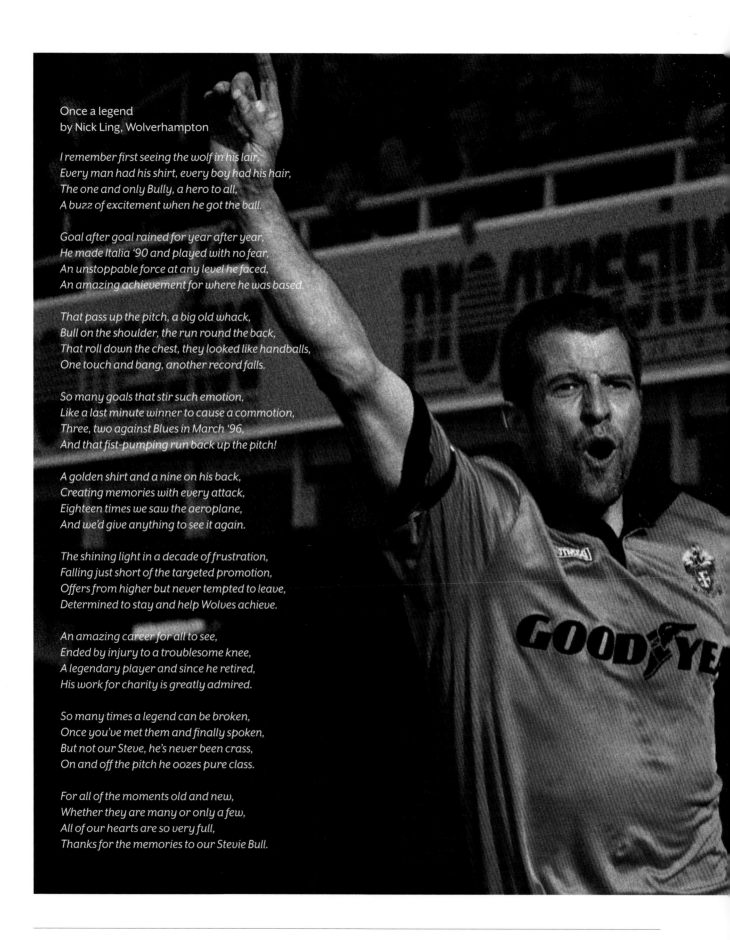

Once a legend
by Nick Ling, Wolverhampton

I remember first seeing the wolf in his lair,
Every man had his shirt, every boy had his hair,
The one and only Bully, a hero to all,
A buzz of excitement when he got the ball.

Goal after goal rained for year after year,
He made Italia '90 and played with no fear,
An unstoppable force at any level he faced,
An amazing achievement for where he was based.

That pass up the pitch, a big old whack,
Bull on the shoulder, the run round the back,
That roll down the chest, they looked like handballs,
One touch and bang, another record falls.

So many goals that stir such emotion,
Like a last minute winner to cause a commotion,
Three, two against Blues in March '96,
And that fist-pumping run back up the pitch!

A golden shirt and a nine on his back,
Creating memories with every attack,
Eighteen times we saw the aeroplane,
And we'd give anything to see it again.

The shining light in a decade of frustration,
Falling just short of the targeted promotion,
Offers from higher but never tempted to leave,
Determined to stay and help Wolves achieve.

An amazing career for all to see,
Ended by injury to a troublesome knee,
A legendary player and since he retired,
His work for charity is greatly admired.

So many times a legend can be broken,
Once you've met them and finally spoken,
But not our Steve, he's never been crass,
On and off the pitch he oozes pure class.

For all of the moments old and new,
Whether they are many or only a few,
All of our hearts are so very full,
Thanks for the memories to our Stevie Bull.

Contents

INTRODUCTION

Stephen George Bull...a name that will forever be synonymous with Wolverhampton Wanderers.

A name that conjures up unforgettable, evocative and cherished memories for thousands and thousands of people.

Steve to his mates, Bully to his fans; this is a man who almost single-handedly transformed the fortunes of an entire football club.

The Backstreet International, The Tipton Terrier, Woolly Bully, The King, or even 'God'...whatever you know him by, Bully's influence travels far and wide.

His footballing exploits – 306 Wolves goals, 18 hat-tricks, 50 goals in two consecutive seasons, going from a builders' yard to a World Cup in just a few short years, to name just a few – are unlikely to ever be matched.

The words 'legend' and 'hero' get tossed around like confetti in football these days – Bully is unquestionably both of those things.

But his almost unique relationship with the club runs deeper than that. Bully is the soul of Wolverhampton Wanderers.

Billy Wright and Stan Cullis may have won more titles and cups, Derek Parkin may have worn the famous gold shirt on more occasions, but Bully elicited worship of almost religious proportions from the adoring Wolves supporters.

He was one of them. They supported him almost as much as they supported the club. And he repaid them with loyalty – and goals.

It's rare you'll find someone so adored who remains so humble. But Bully, despite being just about the most famous man in Wolverhampton, with an MBE fixed to his name and a stand at Molineux named after him, has always greeted each of his achievements with typical modesty.

Since retirement his charity work and his generosity have touched the lives of people just as much as his goals did all those years ago.

And with his association with Wolves now reaching the milestone of 30 years, it seems an appropriate time to reflect on a quite remarkable three decades, both on and off the football field.

Over the next 144 pages you'll read Bully telling the famous story in his own words, with a little help from his family, friends, team mates and fans. It's quite a tale.

Here's to the next 30 years...

FOREWORD
BY GRAHAM TURNER

The hardest thing in football is, without question, scoring goals. In Steve Bull, Wolves discovered one of the best in their history.

306 goals in 561 games for Wolves speaks volumes for his ability to execute the art of goalscoring.

It is a privilege for me to be writing the foreword for this publication celebrating 30 years of Steve's association with our great club.

I first saw Steve play in a Full Members Cup match for West Bromwich Albion at The Hawthorns. To say he was raw was an understatement. However, he had one major attribute which stood out – his desire to get into goalscoring positions.

Nothing stood in his way. He chased lost causes, knocked defenders out of the way and that great desire to hit the back of the net was there for all to see.

A few weeks later, along with Andy Thompson, he became a Wolves player.

It wasn't long before his goalscoring exploits hit the headlines and that led to international recognition with the England Under-21s, England 'B' and then finally, full international honours under the astute management of one of the best England managers there has been - Bobby Robson.

Everyone at the club took immense pride in his selection for the England World Cup squad at Italia 90.

I feel sure that during this period Steve was courted by a number of clubs in the top flight. But his spiritual home was and still is, Molineux.

This loyalty led to the adulation he deservedly received from so many supporters and he remains, to this day, a great Ambassador for Wolves.

I must also mention a short time away from Molineux and a great favour carried out for me personally.

I had bought the shareholding in Hereford United, a club in a dire financial position and recently relegated from the Football League. He joined us, helping me out with the coaching and turning out on the pitch in half a dozen matches.

It is the mark of the man that his old manager wanted some help and, unstintingly, he answered the call. I will never forget that generosity of spirit.

I am occasionally asked, who was the best player that I managed?

There have been some very good ones.

But to me, the best of the lot at doing his job, in Steve's case putting the ball in the back of the net, was undoubtedly Bully.

It has been an association between the club and player that has now lasted 30 years.

Wolves and Bully – clearly a match made in heaven.

Graham Turner.

1986

Thirty years seems a very long time ago and a long time ago it was! So what was the world like the day Steve Bull and Andy Thompson got into that orange Ford Cortina to make the short trip down the M6 from The Hawthorns to Molineux. Let's take a step back in time... and remember.

WHAT THE WORLD WAS LIKE IN NOVEMBER, 1986

Number one in the charts was Berlin's '*Take My Breath Away*', the theme from the film Top Gun, which had been released in the UK the previous month.

Ronald Reagan was five years into his eight-year term as President of the United States of America.

Prime Minister of the UK was Margaret Thatcher, seven years into her 11-year Premiership.

Average house prices in the UK were around £36,000.

Wolves were ninth in the Fourth Division table, having taken 23 points from their first 16 games.

The First Division championship went to Liverpool for the 16th time in their history.

Reigning Wimbledon champions in tennis were Boris Becker and Martina Navratilova.

Mike Tyson won his first boxing world title by defeating Trevor Berbick.

Stephen King's *'It'* book was one of the biggest selling books of the time.

Films released included Star Trek IV The Voyage Home and The Mosquito Coast.

Dennis Potter's critically acclaimed television serial The Singing Detective made its debut on BBC 1.

Beadle's About, which was to run for ten years, was aired for the first time on ITV.

Current Wolves goalkeeper Carl Ikeme was five months old!

Alex Ferguson was appointed Manager of Manchester United.

The most popular toy being bought for Christmas was a Laser Tag.

Prince Andrew and Sarah Ferguson were married at Westminster Abbey.

A large loaf of bread was roughly 33p, pint of milk 23p and pint of beer 75p.

And, of course, 'them up the road' made a big mistake...

AND SO
IT BEGINS...

It's November 1986...a bright-eyed 21-year-old Black Country lad is looking to make a name for himself in professional football.

It's been a dream of his since he was a child and he's now swapped life in a factory for life on a football pitch.

He scored goals for fun in the non-leagues and has made the leap to the pro ranks with a First Division team.

Things are – he thinks – going well. But he's about to be discarded in what looks like a backwards move in his burgeoning career.

However the 10-mile journey down the road would, in time, end up being the best move Stephen George Bull ever made in his career.

Little does he know, but in less than four years he'll be a household name across the country, a World Cup semi-finalist and the biggest cult hero that Wolverhampton Wanderers has ever known.

But back to November 1986, when Bully and his mucker Andy Thompson found themselves in what could kindly be described as rather inauspicious surroundings at a club that was on its knees, experiencing the worst period in its long and illustrious history.

The man himself takes up the story...

"TWO DODGY HAIRCUTS..."

"

"Me and Thommo drove to Molineux in my orange Ford Cortina. We arrived at what looked like a run down shack! We both thought the same: 'What have we done?'. It was shocking - worse than Tipton! (Joke!)

There was one girl on reception, then Keith Pearson who was Club Secretary and Dot Wooldridge. There were basically a handful of people running the club then - absolutely unbelievable.

They told us where to go and we walked down the corridor. The tiles were hanging down from the ceiling and the floor was soaking wet – the place was in a right state.

We stood either side of gaffer Graham Turner's door, he walked out and said "Right, who is first?".

Well Thommo being Thommo, what with his small man syndrome went in first. He was in and out in three minutes. I asked him what he'd signed for, he said £125 a week and a signing on fee.

Then it's my turn, in I go - Graham tells me what's happening. He made it clear they didn't want me up the road. I signed for £200 a week - a striker's wage. And a bit more signing on as well.

But it certainly wasn't about the money at all.

Graham said he was going to give me a chance. I had a medical and there was a bit of a foreign body in my knee, but they said not to worry about it and that if it was a problem they'd fetch it out. As long as I was fit they were going to take a gamble on me.

So that was that, all done, signed. Next we went to watch us play Chorley in the cup and that was absolutely shocking. What had we let ourselves in for?"

Wolves drew that game 1-1 with non-league Chorley. They would lose the second replay – a game Bully was ineligible for – 3-0 and suffer arguably the single biggest humiliation in their history.

With the club also in the bottom division of English football for the first time, the situation had hit rock bottom.

A far cry from the club Bully had just left – West Bromwich Albion (you may also know them as Sandwell Town).

"We had left a club who'd only just been relegated to the Second Division at the time and now we are at a club languishing in the Fourth Division.

I didn't even want to leave the Albion. I'd just broke into the first team, scored three in five games and thought I'd landed.

Me and Thommo got on with everyone in the dressing room. He was from Featherstone and I was from Tipton - we didn't talk posh like our team mates.

Ally Robertson took us under his wing at Albion and he would end up following us to Wolves.

Ron Saunders (Albion Manager) just called me in one day and asked me if I was enjoying it, I said yes. To be honest after scoring three in five I thought he might give me a pay rise!

He basically just said I hadn't got a first touch in that division and that I'd got to go down the road with Thommo. I asked when and he said 'right now'.

At that point there was no question of not signing for Wolves. Me and Thommo were Black Country lads who just wanted to play football.

I just thought I'd take a gamble. We didn't know whether Wolves were going down or up. Yes they were bottom of the Fourth Division, but it was just about playing football.

We didn't look back."

"ANYONE SEEN THOMMO?? ONLY JUST GOT HERE AND LOST HIM ALREADY!"

"One was working in a bed factory called Vono, in Dudley Port, earning £27.50 a week. I left there and went to a builders' yard, Willner Building Supplies in Tipton. I didn't last long there (can't say why!)

Then I went to a warehouse, Dom Holdings in Hill Top, working 14 hours a day.

The football teams I played for were Tipton Town, Red Lion and Newey Goodman – three games a weekend. They were on Saturday mornings, Saturday afternoons and Sunday mornings. It's scary looking back but that's the way it was.

I'm not sure what my goal record was. I started when I was 14. I was playing with the blokes then and I think that helped me mature a bit more.

When you're playing non league football they're chopping you, kicking you, punching you, the whole lot. You just get used to it.

But I was scoring for fun. Alfie Bowman, who was a good midfielder with Newey Goodman, was trying to scout me out all over the place.

No one really honed my game, there was no coaching until I got to Tipton Town. They just let me get on with it, it was natural. You can't teach a goalscorer to score goals – offside traps, the runs, the channels, it's all natural instinct.

I never thought I'd actually play professionally to be honest but Sid Day, who was a scout, knew Johnny Giles and Nobby Stiles at the Albion at the time and recommended me.

I went to the intermediates on Tuesday and Thursday nights to train and then Albion took me on.

Nobby Stiles and Johnny Giles left and then Ron Saunders came in. I played loads for the intermediates and reserves and was scoring plenty of goals so he gave me a chance in the first team.

I scored two against Ipswich at home (in September 1986), we lost 4-3, Paul Cooper was in goal. Then we played Derby in the League Cup two weeks later – we lost 4-1 and I scored one.

But that was it, they didn't want me so I was sold."

Going back a few steps, Bully had first come to prominence a few years earlier after starring in non-league football – playing for three different clubs at the same time.

He combined that with his normal day job. Of which, before making it professionally, he had three...

"AY MUTCHY - THAT'S MY SHIRT....."

Things started slowly for Bully at Wolves. His first ever appearance in the famous gold and black came on November 22, 1986 in a 3-0 home defeat to Wrexham. With him, Thommo and Turner in place, though, the foundations had been laid for what would be a remarkable rise.

"To be honest I can't really remember the first game. My first goal was away at Cardiff in the Freight Rover Trophy (a 1-0 win on December 2). Their centre half was Boyle, it was a header. He chased me all over the park - I jumped for the ball and caught his eye with my finger then scored.

I had the number 8 shirt first, Mutchy (Andy Mutch) had number nine.

I didn't get to wear the number 9 shirt until Mutchy got injured. I hung onto it and when Mutchy was fit again he took number 10.

Nothing really stands out in that first season. The first thing was survival, because they were in liquidation, being sold, they'd dropped down the leagues, so it was all about staying up that season. Then we went on a bit of a run and got into the play-offs where we lost to Aldershot.

It was totally different to Albion. It was spick and span there, Albion had money and Wolves didn't.

Let me tell you, they were not the best dressing rooms. We had a ball block where you'd slam the ball against it, one set of weights, two benches, four baths which had tiles coming off and dirty water. We had two pairs of boots to last us a season.

But we fitted right in. Me and Thommo sat together. All the players used to pick on Thommo and I'd chase them around the dressing room!

From early on we had some good times and we were all good mates.

From 1986 to about 1992 was the best team spirit I've ever known. Everybody stuck together. We drank together, played cards together on the coach, all that stuff.

We were allowed out on the Tuesday afternoon. It was called the Tuesday Club. We used to go to the Odd Spot in Birmingham. We'd run our socks off all morning, the gaffer would make us sick because he knew what we were going to do.

Then it was straight over there in taxis and all the gaffer said was don't bring any trouble back to Wolverhampton. We'd have Wednesday off and then were back in on Thursday.

When we got out of Wolverhampton, we all stuck together. There wasn't a single fight, just a few disagreements here and there.

Me and Mutchy hit it off pretty instantly. I couldn't see him but I could hear him! He was really loud in the changing room. Him and Cooky (Paul Cook). All the jokes we used to tell, it was class.

Digger Barnes used to play left back. We were losing 2-0 at home at half time, I'm not sure who against and the gaffer was giving us a right telling off.

Digger had his head down and he's looked up at us and he's got black tape over his teeth! The gaffer just picked some cups up, threw them across the room and said you better get me a f*****g result now. We drew 2-2 or won 3-2.

We all loved having a joke - we would do all types of stuff, like putting Deep Heat in their pants, cut the bottom off people's socks, tie knots in the jackets so you can't get your arms through, all that stuff - stupid stuff. You'd pick on anyone, myself included."

"ONE OF TWO I SCORED AGAINST
LINCOLN IN 1987"

"NICKY CLARKE, JACKIE GALLAGHER AND
MYSELF TRAINING ON THE CARPARK"

Wolves now train in a multi-million pound state-of-the-art facility at Compton Park.

The 1986 Wolves...well, things were a bit different, it's safe to say. They used a variety of venues around the town. And even, notoriously, the Molineux car park...

"Training was a big part of our week. When I first went to Wolves we used to train at the rugby club in Castlecroft, for a short period of time before we moved onto Dunstall Race course. Graham would make us run round the outside of the track.

Then after Dunstall we went to Wombourne Hockey Club in Pendeford Lane where Jack and Olive Carr used to do food for us – minced beef and dumplings.

But the crazy one was the Wolves car park. It was certainly an eye-opener!

Graham started it off. On a Friday morning, before a Saturday game, wherever you were playing, whatever you did, we had to train on the car park.

There's grit, gravel, bricks, cars...and we're playing football.

We had to shift the cars out of the way before we started and the alarms were going off. All we did was put two cones at either end, that was it. But we never had any injuries at all. Just a bit of grit in your hand.

Everyone was still flying into tackles, falling over, rolling over, it was proper. Tell you what, you wouldn't see players doing that now.

We made it fun. We had the yellow jersey – the gaffer would mark on the chalk board who was the worst player and they'd have to wear it.

In the end we got an Albion top instead. Graham Turner actually got it the one time but refused to wear it!

After the car park we played on the pitch, did a bit of shadow work, set pieces etc. then either got on the coach to travel or went home.

I've no idea why he did it, but it worked. It was eight or nine-a-side, wearing tracksuit bottoms, maybe we did it once and we won, so we kept it going.

The fans used to stand down the sides and they'd help us with the cars as well. Over the weeks the cars were getting sparser and sparser because we kept hitting them."

1988

Things started to snowball rapidly from the 1987/88 season both for Bully and the club.

Wolves won the Division 4 title – and the Sherpa Van Trophy at Wembley – in that season before romping to the Division 3 title in 1988/89. And Bully produced the best goalscoring form of his illustrious career – or indeed of most players' careers.

In 1987/88 he found the net no fewer than 52 times in 58 matches and then the following year, to prove it was certainly no fluke, Bully scored 50 times in 55 games. That meant 102 goals in two years – an astonishing feat.

"It was absolutely stupid. Every time I touched the ball I thought I was going to score. That's not being big-headed, it's just how I felt.

The gaffer said to me, that's your goal in front of you, just hit them hard and they'll go in. I don't remember it starting, it just happened.

Eventually the gaffer started telling me to use my left foot. I watched the video of my goals a few years ago and I scored loads with my left foot. That was my standing leg before then!

It was all just totally unreal in that first season and then the Sherpa Van topped it off – what an experience that was at Wembley. There were 50,000 Wolves fans in a packed Wembley. All I hear from that day are good stories, from our fans and the Burnley fans.

It was a happy, friendly day. The fans were playing football on the car park against each other outside. And when we won it was just superb. I did have a pug on that night though because I didn't score! I think I scored in every round and then I set Mutchy up for his goal in the final but that didn't satisfy me. I wanted to score at Wembley. But I didn't even get a chance on the day. They had Davis and Gardner at the back and I think they were keeping tabs on me more than anyone else.

It was certainly a relaxed build-up to the game.

The week before we went to Santa Ponsa for a break. We trained hard but would also enjoy ourselves with a few beers, even the Gaffer.

One day during training we noticed Graham had his shades on and was just standing back while we were training, not saying much. 'What's the matter gaffer'? I asked 'Hay fever' he replied. 'Yeah right!' I thought!

I know Wolves haven't won much in the last 30 years but the Sherpa Van was a brilliant day for the club, it helped put us back on the map. The crowds started coming back then too. To have 1,500 for home games in 1985 and 1986 and then take 50,000 to Wembley in 1988 shows how much the club was lifted in a short space of time.

Jack Harris and Dick Homden and the rest, they all stuck by the club and it started to grow. Jack Harris was a lovely man, very well-spoken. Him and Dick Homden put the money in from their own pockets for me and Thommo I think, not the club, it was them personally.

I hope they got their money back! You'd see them around the club all the time, they were on the team bus sat at the front. They were very good people and helped make the club what it became in a short space of time."

"THE START OF WOLVES' REVIVAL...
GREAT TEAM SPIRIT"

"OLD WEMBLEY. UNBELIEVABLE. UNFORGETTABLE."

"SHERPA VAN AND THE LEAGUE IN THE
SAME YEAR - WHO'D HAVE KNOWN?"

"OLD RIVALS - I ALWAYS WANTED TO SCORE AGAINST THEM."

Wolves' promotion into Division 2 came with the chance for Bully to lock horns with the old enemy – West Bromwich Albion – the club that had discarded him three years earlier.

In a typically Bully fashion he produced a magical moment, scoring a late winner at the Hawthorns to give Wolves a 2-1 victory in front of their ecstatic fans.

It was a moment that no Wolves supporter in attendance will ever forget.

"It's a goal I will always remember. In the last minute as well! I think that was a sort of 'you're one of us' from the Wolves fans who just went absolutely crazy when I scored.

I got stick from Albion fans from day one. And to this day I will say 'I didn't leave Albion, they sold me. Ron Saunders sold me. I didn't want to leave'.

After leaving all I could do was prove myself and that included scoring as many goals as possible when we played them.

To this day I can shut my eyes and remember the moment. All that green fencing in front of the Smethwick End. Stuart Naylor in goal. Mutchy puts the cross in. I chested it down and hit it and then all of a sudden it was like wild animals in the crowd! Everyone jumping up and down – unbelievable.

We celebrated, kicked off again and the final whistle went. That was it. What a moment."

They were wild times on the pitch – and occasionally wild off it, too.

The players were on their best behaviour most of the time, but there was one occasion in particular when Bully admits he probably took things a step too far...

"Well basically there was one time I should have died, when we were on tour in Austria. The gaffer said to us 'right you've done all your work, now go and have a few beers'.

We're on this mini island and there was a small bay close by where the nightclub was. There was only one way to get there - by this boat. We thought we'd give it a go.

We got across and it's the dodgiest club you've ever seen. It's like 'choose your weapons' when you get in and there was sawdust all over the floor.

We're having a few beers, it's 3 o'clock in the morning, we were all throwing stupid shapes and then it's time to go – and we've got to take the boat back...

Kevin Ashley says to me, 'come on, let's swim back'. It's only 100 yards away, but the tide was going the other way. We'd had a skinful, we get down to our sloggies, stood on the edge of the boat...bang, jumped straight in.

Kevin Ashley jumps in and says 'I ay having this' and climbs straight out. I start swimming but I'm going the wrong way with the tide, out to sea.

I was really struggling and I went under three times, gasping for air, it's not looking good. The fourth time, I don't know if it was Cooky or someone, grabbed me, pulled my sloggies right up my backside and dragged me out!

I know I could have drowned that night. Another 20 seconds and I probably would have done.

I thought I could do it because I'd had a skinful. We didn't tell the gaffer, that's for sure!"

"CELEBRATING WITH PAUL DARBY, GRAHAM
AND THOMMO IN THE BACKGROUND"

"EARLY DAYS WITH JOHN PASKIN,
THOMMO AND DENNO"

It was a different time to be a footballer.

Players were allowed the odd drink and not even legends like Billy Wright would complain at their behaviour, as Bully explains...

"They give you these bags or cases to take all your stuff in for your trip when you're on pre-season.

Well what me and Thommo did, we emptied our bag and filled it up with Carling. We go to this place and it had little chalets on the outside. That was our accommodation.

We took everything out of the mini-bar and put our beers in. (It's pre-season, remember - this is the last thing we should be doing!)

Anyway, we're there one day chilling out in our room and realised our neighbour was Billy Wright! Class!

We had been watching MTV 24/7 for three nights, full blast. We hear a knock on the door in the middle of the night. I got up to see who it was: 'oh hello Bill, how you doing?!' I said. "Erm...Steve...I'm just trying to get to sleep, can you turn the telly down a bit?" 'Ok Bill, no worries at all'. We shut the door and then turn the telly down - just a little bit.

At training the next morning Billy Wright comes over sheepishly and says "Steve, I'd just like to apologise for knocking your door last night."

'No worries Bill, same time tonight?!' That was the gentleman he was."

Wolves couldn't quite make it three promotions in a row, finishing 10th in Division 2 in 1989/90. But for Bully life had changed beyond all recognition from when he first stepped foot inside the shack that was Molineux in 1986.

His status as a hero of the Molineux masses was assured...and he was getting national attention too, which soared around the time of the 1990 World Cup when the 'Backstreet International' became a household name.

Just how much did his life change in those short few years?

"It's weird. To this day, I still think of it as 'wow I was getting paid to do this as my job.'

I do love the adulation, I still love it when they sing my songs at games today. In those days it was just doing your job, then going out for a few beers, job done.

Don't forget, we used to mingle with the supporters, go down the Goalpost on a night-time, it was so very different to today.

When we got together down Eves nightclub with the fans, it was just normal. That's the one thing I wouldn't change. You can't do that now as a footballer, you can't even blow your nose anymore without someone taking a picture of you on their phone.

I didn't mind being recognised at all. We were all down to earth people, we were a unit, not individuals. The supporters recognised that. There were no phones - the only ones we had were those massive ones with an aerial!

We'd be in the Pigot Arms all dressed as Elvis for our Christmas do. You wouldn't do that now. They were great days."

Bully's goals soon attracted the attention of the rest of the country – and the national team. Call-ups to the England B team and the Under-21 team (featuring as an overage player) gave him a taste of international football.

His Wolves strike partner Andy Mutch joined him on a couple of occasions, as did hundreds of giddy Wolves supporters who would follow Bully wherever he went, supporting him almost as much as they did the club.

Then, in May 1989, came the big one – Bully was called up by the full England squad. It made Bully just the fifth post-war player (and still the most recent) to play for England while plying his trade outside the top two divisions. It wasn't just for any game either...this was Scotland away, at Hampden Park.

"I was in the under-21s in Scandinavia somewhere...I went to bed at about 8pm that night and Dave Sexton knocked the door, someone had come down with flu and Bobby Robson wanted me in Scotland for the senior squad at Royal Troon Golf Club.

I had to go right there and then – by 5am I'd arrived. It was like Christmas at the hotel – in your room you've got boots, golf clubs, trainers, tracksuits, the lot. I slept for a couple of hours, got up and then Bobby introduced me to all the players. I shook hands with all of them and then before I know it I'm on the coach going to training with Gary Lineker, Peter Beardsley, Chris Waddle, Paul Gascoigne and Peter Shilton. I was so nervous.

I could deal with the under-21s and live with them. But then you get to the senior squad and you're wondering what you're doing there. I didn't know what to think. But training went really well and I soon settled in. And then in the game itself I couldn't get my hat on. I rang my mum and told her to put ten bob in the back of the telly. We go to the ground and there's about 65,000 people - 60,000 Jocks, 5,000 England fans....I look in the corner and there's a load of Wolves fans. I couldn't believe they'd come to see me.

I was sat on the bench and still wondering what I was doing there. The game's going on and then, quite early on, John Fashanu goes down, so Bobby tells me to warm up. But I'm still not thinking I'll be going on. Fashanu gets back up so I'm back in the pit sitting down.

Ten minutes later Fashanu goes down again, I'm back out for another warm up. Then Bobby shouts for me – I'm coming on. Fashanu walks towards me, we smack hands and he wishes me all the best.

Then about 10 minutes from the end, I think it was Gary Stevens at right back, ball goes forward, I bounce off Dave McPherson, the ball hits me on the shoulder and drops perfect, I just hit it, bang.

All I could see was a microphone in the corner of the goal and it hits that. I'd scored, unbelievable. I started running - and ran towards the Jocks! What was I doing. It was absolutely surreal and amazing."

With football in 1989 consumed very differently to how it is today, with no internet or mobile phones and little TV coverage, little was known of Bully across the land despite him netting 100 goals in two seasons.

But the Scotland debut strike made the nation curious as to the origins of this 'backstreet international', as Bully was dubbed.

Within a year there would be a national campaign for him to start in the World Cup. For now, though, Bully was keeping his feet firmly on the ground.

"It was all over the place after the Scotland game. Old fashioned centre forward, Black Country lad, Roy of the Rovers etc.

The Wolves lads went away and they were watching it at the airport. Thommo said they couldn't believe it.

Things just carried on as normal for me though. Graham Turner kept my feet on the ground saying my bread and butter was at Wolves, I wouldn't be playing for England if I wasn't playing well for Wolves.

It didn't go massive like it might do today. Wolves wanted to keep me here and there was a lot of speculation, so the club gave me a half decent contract at that point.

I wasn't a greedy person, they offered me a fair deal. It was very rare I went in to speak to them about a contract. I think my first pay rise was £50 a week, after that first season, for scoring 19 goals."

The England call-ups continued. Bully again came on as a substitute in a friendly away at Denmark, before starting at Wembley against Yugoslavia in December 1989.

It was during his second start though, that Bully confirmed he belonged at that level and staked a huge claim for the World Cup squad, when he scored twice against Czechoslovakia at Wembley in a 4-2 win in April 1990.

The first was a stunning half volley after he expertly chested down Gascoigne's through ball, the second a bullet header into the roof of the net from a Gascoigne cross.

"Gazza certainly knew where I was that day! It was like Paul Cook was doing at Wolves – he'd put it on a plate for me; chest, head, foot – goal.

You did feel different, you're playing with Waddle, Gascoigne, Pop Robson. You don't think you've got the nation on your shoulders though, you don't realise at all.

You just put your blinkers on and forget about things like that. You do feel special putting that England shirt on though. I didn't take it all in to be fair, it was a game and I was playing, simple as that.

Wembley was a different thing altogether, one of the biggest and oldest stadiums in the world. It was very daunting. To go there and score as well, that's even better. I had a taste of it in 1988 and had no idea I'd be there a couple of years later scoring for England."

The clamour for Bully's inclusion in Bobby Robson's World Cup squad was huge.

A further 27 goals in 48 games in the Second Division in 1989/90, plus those three strikes for England, convinced Robson to 'let the Bull loose', as pundit Jimmy Greaves would famously call for in a t-shirt he wore on national television.

And of course he got the nod. A 26-man squad was whittled down to 22 and Bull was selected ahead of Arsenal striker Smith.

"Graham Turner was the one who told me about the World Cup call-up. I wasn't confident about being picked, you don't expect that. You had Lineker, Beardsley, Cottee, Fashanu, Alan Smith, Merson, Ian Wright, there were loads of great strikers.

Bobby Robson said the reason he took me was because none of the teams knew who I was. He believed in me, he knew what I could do.

He was a great bloke and a great man manager. Him and Don Howe, the pair of them together were a superb team.

Bobby always used to say, whatever you do, don't change what you do for Wolves and you'll do well.

He said 'run at them, get at them and frighten the life out of them and they'll be scared of you'."

After the World Cup tournament Bully returned for club duty still as determined as ever to add some top flight experience to the international caps which were a source of pride to everyone connected with Wolves.

World Cup hangover? Not exactly.

Bully notched a brace on the opening day against Oldham at a sunny Molineux– sadly Oldham striker Ian Marshall notched three.

He averaged a goal a game in the first 13 league fixtures, including a hat-trick against Bristol City which took him to double figures for trebles.

Still that top flight ambition burned and burned bright for him at Molineux, but there was plenty of frustration as Wolves just couldn't make that final, crucial step.

And Bull sensed a shift in emphasis in the dressing room in the early Nineties.

The success forged on the foundations of team spirit and good, old fashioned hard work had laid the groundwork for a push for the Premier League.

But now Wolves needed more.

Sir Jack Hayward had checked in at the helm and was now carrying out a much-needed sprucing up of a stadium in need of modernising and a facelift.

Sir Jack also invested not only in the infrastructure, but also in the team and higher profile players started to arrive.

"Something started to change a bit in the 1990s. Some players came in on big money and it changed the mood of the dressing room.

The old players were maybe thinking about what money they were on and comparing it to what the new lads were getting.

I wouldn't say it was negative or anything, just one of those things that happens at a club.

Some of the players were getting a bit niggled, but it did settle down again once the club realised they needed to look after the players who had been there a while.

And the quality of the players coming in increased as well.

Steve Froggatt, Tony Daley, Geoff Thomas – players like that coming in gave us the impression Wolves were wanting to go places.

We gave it a really good go, but had some bad luck, particularly with injuries and couldn't take that crucial final step."

"MY FIRST GLAMOUR SHOOT..."

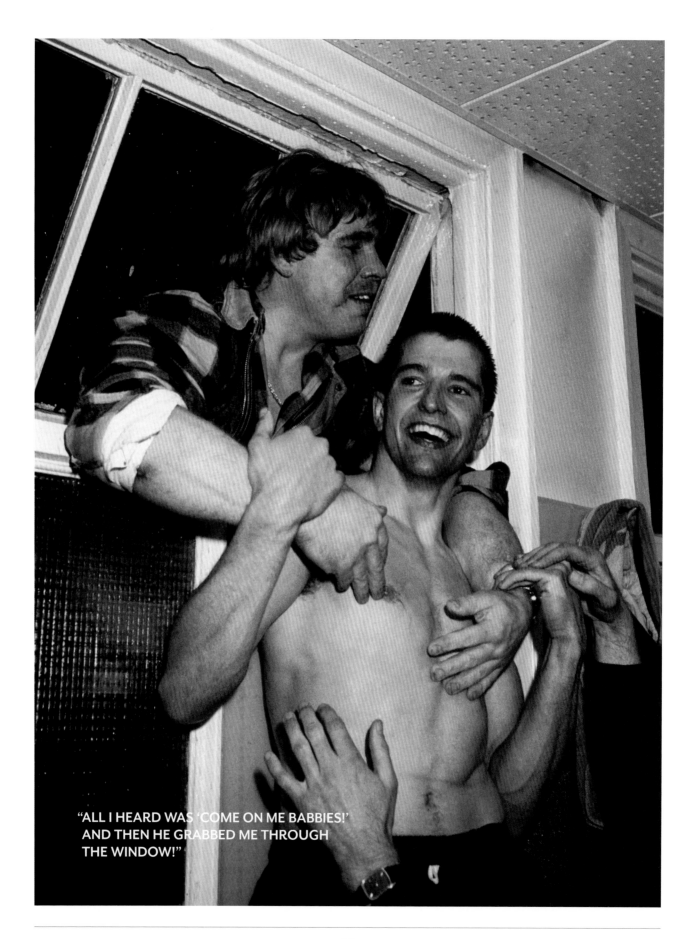

"ALL I HEARD WAS 'COME ON ME BABBIES!'
AND THEN HE GRABBED ME THROUGH
THE WINDOW!"

"ME POLITELY EXPLAINING TO MY WEST HAM FRIENDS THAT I DIDN'T FEEL I'D GONE IN TOO HARD ON THEIR KEEPER AND THAT HE WAS LUCKY I DIDN'T GO IN HARDER...!"

On reaching what was then the Second Division in 1989 following successive promotions, Wolves finished 10th, 12th, 11th, 11th and 8th.

Then came a fourth placed finish in 1994/95, leading to a play-off semi final with Bolton.

And a dramatic and electrically charged evening which remains etched in the mindsets of all Wolves fans who witnessed it.

Dateline May 17th, 1995. Three days earlier Wolves had earned themselves a 2-1 first leg lead against the other Wanderers, courtesy of Bull and Mark Venus.

The advantage should have been greater, only for evergreen visiting keeper Peter Shilton to roll back the years with a string of top class saves.

Then came the second leg. Ouch!

"Bolton in the play-offs was one of the lowest times of my career. We really thought we were going to do it that year.

Goals were flying in, the team spirit was right up there and if we didn't get there it wasn't going to be for the want of trying. We were up there, flying high and thinking we were going to make it.

We won the first leg 2-1 but should have won by more – they had Peter Shilton diving all over the place keeping shots out left right and centre. When we played the second leg we still fancied our chances the way we had been playing.

It just turned into one of those nights. They beat us and it was one of the lowest points of my career. We just weren't quite strong enough to get over the line."

There was a lot more to it than just the result.

With the game finely poised, Bolton striker John McGinlay appeared to aim a punch at David Kelly, in an incident which earns McGinlay a special Wolves welcome any time he is in the area!

One of the more iconic images of the Wolves legend is of Bully sat on the pitch, head bowed, in silent and utterly painful contemplation.

For those present at Burnden Park, that image seemed to go on for hours.

"How was I feeling at that moment? Probably not a word I can repeat in this book. I was thinking we had come so far, worked our socks off and it was that Scottish, that Scottish, person John McGinlay and Bolton again, who had done us.

I was sat on the floor for what seemed like an eternity, I couldn't get my head around it. But then we all picked ourselves up, got back in the changing rooms and the gaffer told us we had given it our best shot.

There was a lot of anger in there and a lot of people boiling up inside. It wasn't like the players wanted to fight anyone – more just this anger and frustration that people needed to let out. We felt we should have won it, we should have been going on to the final.

We had a couple of drinks in the dressing room, got on the bus and went home.

The gaffer (*Graham Taylor*) had us in for a meeting the next day, then told us to go off on holiday and be ready to go again when we came back."

"FROM THIS..."

"...TO THIS..."

51

There was another play-off failure to follow, against Crystal Palace at the end of the 1996/97 season.

As ever with Wolves, it was accompanied by a dollop of painstaking drama, almost black humour.

A goal down in the last minute of the first leg, Palace's later-to-be-Wolves striker Dougie Freedman made it two, only for Wolves' later-to-be-Palace defender Jamie Smith to respond immediately.

A 2-1 deficit would have left the tie beautifully poised, but yet there were still enough seconds of added time remaining for Freedman to add another. 3-1. Palace in the pound seats.

The second leg witnessed one of the most electrically charged Molineux atmospheres of a generation, hordes of passionate fans imploring their heroes to pull off an unlikely comeback.

It didn't happen. Mark Atkins' early goal was cancelled out by David Hopkin. Ady Williams scored a second goal for Wolves to make it 2-1 but it was not enough to overturn the deficit from the first leg.

Another near miss. More heroic failure. Wolves appeared to have the patent for it.

There were still a couple more seasons left for Bull after the Palace. And here was when new faces started to emerge.

Lee Naylor, Matt Murray, Joleon Lescott, Keith Andrews – there were bright lights emerging from the Molineux youth ranks with quantity and quality not seen for many a year.

Not to mention a young Irish fella who joined the club at 15 and who, within two years, was scoring a brace on his debut on the opening day of the season at Norwich.

"Oh yes, Robbie Keane. Class player, brilliant player and a selfish player, bit like myself. That is what strikers are like – the good ones anyway!

He was a young lad coming up and I always felt I would be happy to pass my shirt on to him. He was very confident as a young lad, chirpy, always there and ready to pop up with a bit of cheek!

I had to give him the odd 'squeeze' every now and again just to rein him in a little bit, same as with Matt Murray, Keith Andrews and others! You know, just a nice headlock and scrubbing their heads with my fist.

But they all just wanted to play football.

Robbie was frustrating because he would go down the wing nine times, I'd be in the box and he wouldn't put the ball in. I'd give him a right tatering because he should have given me the ball. Then the tenth time I wouldn't be in the box and the ball would go in!

But he was a great player.

He went on to great heights and fair play to him, he's had a brilliant career and it was great to be with him at the start of it."

1996

Bully nuts for Brazil!

"It was a good testimonial game for me against Santos.

We had tried a couple of English clubs such as Newcastle but couldn't get them for the date that we wanted. Jim Cadman, who was running the testimonial year for me, then suggested we should approach some foreign opposition.

Santos were due to visit to play a few games and you can't get much better than taking on the Brazilians can you? All I wanted to make sure was that the fans enjoyed it – which I think they did.

My two boys Jack and Joe walked out onto the pitch with me that day and it was absolutely brilliant. They loved it that day. While it has now been a very long time ago I hope they still remember it and enjoyed going out onto the pitch with their Dad.

The game finished 1-1 with big Don Goodman getting our goal. It was a great day."

"PROUD DAY FOR ME - ONE OF THE FIRST TIMES I LED US OUT AS CAPTAIN... ANYONE FANCY A CUPPA?!"

As Bully advanced in years so too his influence started to change.

He had always been one of the key figures in the dressing room, his unwavering determination, honesty and will to win demanded nothing less.

But now there were young players coming under his tutelage – he was also captain for a time – and it was a role he relished as he knew his playing days could not go on for ever.

"It was nice to be a bit of a father figure to some of those lads at that time. I didn't know how long I would be able to keep going with the knee injuries I had.

But it was nice to be there as an experienced voice and I think they listened every now and again! Hopefully some of what I said maybe helped them out.

I was captain a few times as well. Me being the older statesman to take responsibility.

I always felt a captain should be at the back to be able to see everything going on in front of him but it was still a great honour.

Curley (Keith Curle) was a great captain. Very vocal. Ady Williams as well was also very vocal.

Keith Downing I think was captain once or twice in the early years. A little 'rotter' in the middle of the park snapping at everyone.

I certainly played alongside many good captains and good personalities."

But so it transpired that Bull's talents and body began to wane. No one could play on for ever – not even Stephen George Bull.

But there are so many landmarks to remember his career by, so many incredible moments, when nets were left bulging and supporters open-mouthed.

How do you choose from 306 goals? With great difficulty.

Hereford away is one that remains in the Bull psyche, latching on to an Andy Mutch flick-on before turning and smashing home with his right foot.

Not so full of technique but packed with meaning was one at Derby in March, 1992, number 195 of his Wolves career, overhauling the great John Richards' club record. Number 100 had come against Bristol City, number 200 against Leicester and 300 against Bradford City.

Those England ones of course. The last minute winner at Albion previously mentioned. A last minute winner against Blues, which still raises a smile over two decades on!

"Nothing will ever replicate the feeling of scoring a goal.

I know people will try and compare it to other things. And that is why I loved it so much. Once I scored one, I wanted another. Some players after getting one thought it was job done. Not for me. I always wanted more and more. The feeling is unbelievable.

That one against Blues for example when we beat them 3-2. Always sticks in my mind that one.

At 2-1 down we thought we needed to come back to try and get a draw out of it. We got the equaliser and then Simon Osborn hit a ball over the top. Michael Johnson was centre half and I slipped as I hit the ball and at full stretch, connected with it and it found it's way into the bottom corner.

I think everyone has seen the pictures of me running along the stand then clenching my fist in celebration in front of the Blues fans.

I don't think Barry Fry has ever forgiven me!

I couldn't move at the end of it I was so knackered.

That sort of feeling is unbelievable, the hairs on the back of your neck stand up. Even when I watch it again now.

The emotion that goes through your body is difficult to describe."

"GET IN - 3-2 - BLUES FANS
HERE I COME!!"

1998

"MY LAST GOAL FOR WOLVES.
WHO'D HAVE BELIEVED IT."

The very last of those goals came on September 26th, 1998, against Bury at Molineux.

Kevin Muscat broke down the right and sent over a cross which Bull met at the far post to despatch a low header past Dean Kiely. 306 up and, although no one was to know it at the time, 306 and out.

The man himself was certainly not aware that this would be his final celebration, in front of the North Bank now known as the Stan Cullis Stand.

There were 20,155 there to witness it, equally unaware that the only goal of the game would ultimately become something of a historical one.

That was in the September and with injuries starting to bite, there were only another six Bull appearances to follow in that 1998/99 season.

The fat lady was clearing her throat and yet, on the final day of that campaign when Bull came off the bench to replace Haavard Flo against a Bradford team who finished up celebrating promotion, still no one thought that would be that.

"The header – at the back post. Yes I remember that one. I had been having a few injury problems but I would never have guessed that it would be the last goal of my Wolves career.

If I had then nobody would have caught me – I'd have been running around the pitch like a mad man!

I had some problems during that season but at the end I was still thinking everything was going to be ok. My knee was feeling fine and I just thought I would get myself off for six weeks and then come back ready to go again in pre-season.

But it wasn't to be. I did a couple of weeks which was fine and then the one day it just went crack and I felt the pain.

I sat down with the physio Barry Holmes and we discussed what was best to do.

"He said I could keep having the knee done and try and continue but in the long term it would only get worse.

But he knew how much football meant to me and he said it had to be my decision.

When I thought it might mean problems once I'd finished playing I think that probably made my mind up for me."

A tough decision, but the right decision and one which, for all the memories, Bully wouldn't regret.

Unfortunately, it needed to be done.

"I had to let my head rule my heart. We were on the pre-season tour of Sweden at the time and I made the decision and once I'd said it, then it was done.

I watched the lads finish the tour off, came home and went straight off to hospital to get the knee sorted. When it happened I remember we were just sat there on the steps with Colin Lee and it had all come to an end.

My body was telling me to stop.

I retired at the right time, even though I would have loved to have kept going. I didn't play too long, I just retired when I should have done.

I could probably have carried on, kept taking the money for a few games a season, but I didn't want to do that.

All dreams come to an end sometime and it was a massive decision, because I'd spent all my life playing football. But it was my knees telling me my time was up!

I was 34 and had to tell myself that I'd done my bit and I'd played football for 16 years, it was time to call it a day.

I was still enjoying my football and I did until the very last day. It's every man's dream to go out of the front door and go to training every day, get your boots on and get out there and play football.

And to enjoy the job you are doing.

That's what I did and I've still got the memories, but all good things have to come to an end."

The Wolves playing career may have been at an end, but all the memories of those 306 goals, promotions, Wembley – what a 13 years it had been.

But in many ways the association with Molineux was just on hold, ready to return, in a different guise.

For Bully and Wolves, there were still many more chapters to come.

"THE END OF AN ERA."

Steve Bull and Andy Thompson were the 696th and 697th players to represent Wolves when they made their debuts against Wrexham on November 22nd, 1986.

With thanks to research from statistician and lifelong Wolves fan Scott Pritchard, Wolves programme editor/club historian John Hendley, Wolves Museum curator Pat Quirke and local journalist/author David Instone, here are those players to have turned out for the club during Bully's 13-year playing career.

For the record the last debut-maker of Bully's reign was Haavard Flo, with Darren Bazeley and Andy Sinton the first new arrivals to feature following his retirement.

Over the page Bully has put together not one but two dream Wolves XIs picking from his team-mates. There were many others whom he enjoyed playing alongside but he couldn't squeeze them in to that elite 22!

Chris Brindley	Paul Stancliffe	Darren Ferguson	Jens Dowe
Mark Kendall	Colin Taylor	Guy Whittingham	Richard Leadbeater
Brian Caswell	Mark Blake	Jamie Smith	Adrian Williams
Rob Kelly	Paul Birch	Neil Emblen	Michael Gilkes
Robbie Dennison	Mark Todd	Steve Froggatt	Carl Robinson
Phil Robinson	Mark Burke	Paul Stewart	Darius Kubicki
Keith Downing	Lawrie Madden	Mark Walters	Steve Sedgley
Jackie Gallagher	Derek Mountfield	Tony Daley	Robbie Keane
Nigel Vaughan	Mark Rankine	John De Wolf	Mixu Paatelainen
Gary Bellamy	James Kelly	Don Goodman	Simon Coleman
Bobby McDonald	Paul Blades	Brian Law	Isidro Diaz
Mark Venus	Paul Edwards	Gordan Cowans	Chris Westwood
Phil Chard	Darren Roberts	Jermaine Wright	Jesus Sanjuan
Mick Gooding	Paul Jones (keeper)	Dean Richards	Lee Naylor
Tom Bennett	Dave Beasant	Dennis Pearce	Paul Simpson
Tim Steele	Darren Simkin	Eric Young	Dougie Freedman
Mike Stowell	Shaun Bradbury	Mark Atkins	Kevin Muscat
Roger Hansbury	Mark Turner	Mark Williams	Hans Segers
Tony Lange	Geoff Thomas	Dominic Foley	Robbie Slater
Shane Westley	David Kelly	Simon Osborn	Steve Claridge
John Paskin	Kevin Keen	Vinny Samways	Stephen Wright
Paul McLoughlin	Cyrille Regis	Steve Corica	Fernando Gomez
Paul Cook	Peter Shirtliff	Glen Crowe	David Connolly
Paul Jones (outfield)	Lee Mills	Serge Romano	Mark Jones
Brian Roberts	Mike Small	Iwan Roberts	Ryan Green
Rob Hindmarch	Neil Masters	Keith Curle	Robert Niestroj
Kevin Ashley	Chris Marsden	Robin Van Der Laan	Haavard Flo

BULLY'S WOLVES
DREAM TEAMS

MIKE STOWELL

GOALKEEPER : MIKE STOWELL

What a brilliant keeper Stowelly was. A great shot-stopper. He hated me taking penalties or shots against him in training because I'd smack it hard against his hand

RIGHT BACK : KEVIN MUSCAT

I've got to go for the animal in the team, Kevin Muscat. What an absolute beast he was. He'd take the ball and the man and then the man and the ball again, then he'd put them in the stand and go and kick them again! But off the field he was a nice guy - top drawer. A great character.

KEVIN MUSCAT

CENTRE BACK : DEAN RICHARDS

He was the Alan Hansen of our side, strolling and gliding around the pitch and passing it here, there and everywhere. He'd give you the odd goal as well, a fantastic footballer.

DEAN RICHARDS

CENTRE BACK : KEITH CURLE

Curley was the only man I knew who could smoke cigarettes and play football. He would give you 100 per cent and run himself into the ground. A commanding centre half.

KEITH CURLE

LEFT BACK : ANDY THOMPSON

My old room partner, the flying pig we called him, flying up and down that wing all day long. He scored one or two goals too - 52 penalties or something like that!

ANDY THOMPSON

RIGHT WING : PAUL BIRCH

Like Dean Richards and Mark Kendall, another great player and friend who left us too soon. We used to call him the dwarf, or dungeon master. He was a great, skilful player.

PAUL BIRCH

CENTRAL MIDFIELD : KEITH DOWNING

The Jack Russell, as we called him. Middle of the park, he'd offer anybody out on the pitch even though he was only 3ft high. He'd have a go, leave his foot in, stand up tall to 6ft blokes. A good-spirited man and very important in our team.

KEITH DOWNING

CENTRAL MIDFIELD : PAUL COOK

He could find anybody on the pitch. He'd find me over the top all the time, left side, right side, he could find me on a 10-yard pass or a 50-yard pass. He created plenty of my goals.

PAUL COOK

LEFT WING : ROBBIE DENNISON

A proper tricky winger and like Thommo, another flying pig. He'd come in with the odd tap-in from 30 yards as well! He scored some great goals from free kicks and his deliveries from the flank were superb.

ROBBIE DENNISON

CENTRE FORWARD : ANDY MUTCH

My strike partner. We went on for seven years and caused havoc all over the place. Great player, great man off the field as well.

ANDY MUTCH

CENTRE FORWARD : DAVID KELLY

He was a great player and friend and could score goals all day for Wolves and Ireland. He left a bit too soon but certain things happened at the club. Just a shame he was an Albion fan!

DAVID KELLY

GOALKEEPER : MARK KENDALL

The joker of the pack. A very clever and witty man, but when he went out onto the field he was serious and got the job done.

MARK KENDALL

RIGHT BACK : JAMIE SMITH

We called him 'Jinky' because he'd jink in and out down that right wing and get the ball in the box. They were always quality balls as well.

JAMIE SMITH

CENTRE BACK : JOHN DE WOLF

The beast! With that long hair and being 6ft tall - he was scary! All he had to do was breathe and growl and he'd scare the living daylights out of you. He was a presence in that changing room.

JOHN DE WOLF

CENTRE BACK : FLOYD STREETE

One of the old favourites, another 6ft lad and he was 5ft wide as well. You certainly knew he was on the field - I wouldn't have liked to play against him.

FLOYD STREETE

LEFT BACK : MARK VENUS

He could certainly talk a very good game! Some days he didn't play as well as he talked! No, he was a great player, his sidefoot of the ball was exceptional. He never used his laces, but he'd play a 50-yard pass with his side foot.

MARK VENUS

RIGHT WING : TONY DALEY

He was fast as you like - a knife through butter - and he knew where to put the ball in the box as well. His career was too short, but when he was fit he was quite a player.

TONY DALEY

CENTRAL MIDFIELD : GORDON COWANS

It's very rare you get a talented two-footed player but Spud was one. He could pick you out, dink you in and score goals as well.

GORDON COWANS

CENTRAL MIDFIELD : SIMON OSBORN

Cockney Simon - he was another joker, same height as Keith Downing but he'd chirp and chirp, get at players and slot me in as well. That memorable late winner at home to Blues was one I'll never forget.

SIMON OSBORN

LEFT WING : STEVE FROGGATT

He was the scruffiest man in the changing room! But as a footballer and a man, absolutely brilliant. Another who suffered with injuries, the same as Tony Daley, but he always gave everything on the pitch.

STEVE FROGGATT

CENTRE FORWARD : DON GOODMAN

Another good friend of mine - he could rise like a salmon. He was the arch-rival at Albion but he wore gold and black with pride. We're still good friends, he's a top man.

DON GOODMAN

CENTRE FORWARD : ROBBIE KEANE

Our career paths crossed each other and I only played seven games with him. A very frustrating player in my eyes - he'd go down the wing 10 times and I'd make a run in the box 10 times and he'd never pick me out! But a very skilful player and look at where his career took him.

ROBBIE KEANE

"TWO GREAT TEAMS HERE... PLENTY MORE COULD HAVE GOT IN EASY!"

RETIREMENT

Life after the final whistle of Bully's exceptional playing career

1999

What do you do, when everything you have known for almost a decade-and-a-half, everything you ever dreamt of, suddenly comes to an end?

That was the question confronting Bully when he finally had to admit defeat and hang up his boots in the summer of 1999.

Thirteen years at Wolves, 561 appearances – which puts him third in the all-time appearance list – 306 goals, which is of course top of that particular category and 13 England caps which brought a further four goals.

What do you do? How do you deal with it? As Bully himself recalls, it took some time.

Bully has of course maintained that long and successful association with Wolves, through an ambassadorial role, then the Vice-Presidency and the small matter of having a stand named after him, which took place in 2003.

He admits that came as something of a shock.

"In the first few weeks after retiring I was like 'this is ok', I'll get my knee done, come in for treatment, I'll still be part of the club.

And then it went six weeks, seven weeks, eight weeks – and I started to realise – 'I'm not a footballer any more.'

I would still pop in after that, watch a bit of training, get some ice on my knee and then gradually that would slip back and that would be that.

I had to understand that I'd done my bit, I'd done 16 years, tried my hardest, but that was the end.

I needed to get it all out of my system, I started hitting the golf course a bit more and just passed the time away."

"I couldn't get my head around that. I was at Molineux as we'd got an event going on and Sir Jack told me that he wanted to name a stand after me.

It was a bit tricky for me because I knew it was named after John Ireland but Sir Jack said he wanted to do it for me.

He said I had earned it and with that I had to accept. It was still strange having a stand named after me!

And then the Vice-Presidency as well which is another massive honour. To still be part of Wolves after 30 years and to have that title is something else. It feels like I'm part of the furniture!"

As revealed earlier, Bully admits to being a Liverpool fan growing up.

But clearly his long-standing association with Wolves as player, Ambassador, Vice-President and fan who still watches a lot of matches from the stands, holds far more sway.

He also insists he will always speak out in the best interests of the club, whether things are good, bad or indifferent!

Continuing to be stopped by Wolves fans, to chat with Wolves fans, or pose for photos or sign autographs for Wolves fans, remains something considered by Bully as a huge honour and a privilege.

"I was always an armchair Liverpool supporter but now I'm Wolves through and through. Anyone says anything bad about Wolves – and if it's not fair – then I'm straight on their case!

I will tell it like it is – and if I feel Wolves are doing wrong then I say so. I think you have to and I always say what I think is right for the good of the club.

I will reminisce with fans all day long, but ask me what I did last week and I couldn't tell you.

Talk to me about a goal I scored 20 years ago and I can take you through it again! Usually anyway!

I still love being around the club and being asked for autographs and pictures – I still feel very proud and fortunate to have done what I did.

As they say, it's when people stop wanting to talk to you that you should worry!

I've always tried to be really approachable and to get on with people – that is how I was brought up and it's in my nature."

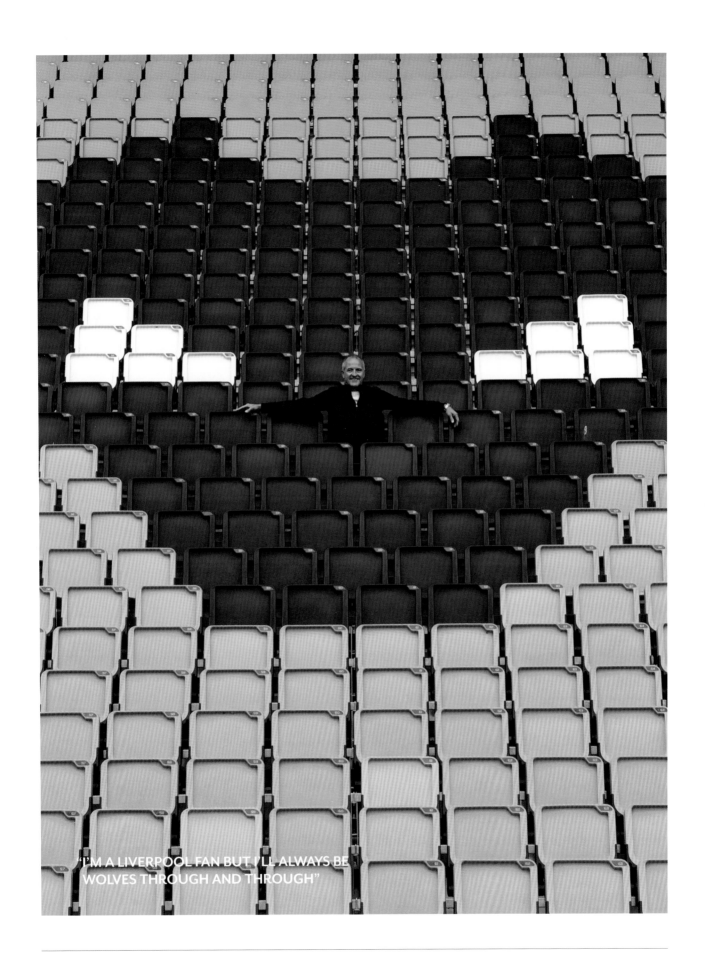

"I'M A LIVERPOOL FAN BUT I'LL ALWAYS BE
WOLVES THROUGH AND THROUGH"

That feeling is certainly mutual. Bully loves the Wolves fans. And the Wolves fans love Bully. Still. After all these years.

It was in the last Millennium that he made his last senior competitive appearance at Molineux – on as a substitute against Bradford City in May, 1999.

And yet, at pretty much every first team match even now, you will more often than not hear Bully's name sung loud and proud by those of a gold and black persuasion.

'Hark now Hear'… 'We'll Drink a Drink'… 'Ooh Bully Bully'…. the songlist remains extensive.

But what does the great man think when he is there at a match, or even if he is watching at home on television and his name drifts across the airwaves?

"It is weird, I get embarrassed and look at my feet! I wonder why it is that they are singing about me.

But again it is a huge privilege. Sometimes I will be watching a game on Sky and I'll hear 'Stevie Bull's a Tatter'.

I never have been a Tatter by the way, I don't know where that came from. But it is great to hear it.

And sometimes when I'm at an away game with my mates as soon as I get spotted it all starts up. We do it now and again, about 16 of us, get on the minibus, arrive at the ground and have a pie and a few beers.

The Wolves fans are just brilliant!

They are there day in day out, through thick and thin, snow, sleet or rain.

It is brilliant to be in there with those fans and I will keep doing it, for half a dozen games a season.

I feel like a proper fan when I am in there in that away end.

I don't mind going in the corporate seats when I'm asked and representing the club. I never take that lightly.

But yes, I really do enjoy being in there with the fans."

There is one photograph which stands out among those of Bully attending Wolves games.

It was at Shrewsbury, in September, 2013 and Bully was attending one of his regular games as a fan with a minibus full of friends.

His mom, Joan, had passed away days earlier and it was an emotional time.

But when the fans implored him to 'give us a song', he duly responded!

"There was that picture from the Shrewsbury game a couple of years ago. I organised the trip, the tickets, the bus, everything. But we ended up with 14 tickets and 15 people!

It was all sold out. I had to be a bit cheeky and went into reception and they recognised me and said 'alright Steve, what's going on?'

I just said all my mates were in there and I didn't really want to go upstairs to the hospitality – I wanted to be in with the fans. The staff were great and they walked me around and into the stand – and I was in there before all the lads got in!

They all wind me up at games and give it the: 'Bully Give us A Song'. So that day I did and it was something about the Albion which I'd better not repeat here!

I didn't really mean it – but everyone started singing it and that was when someone got me with the photo!"

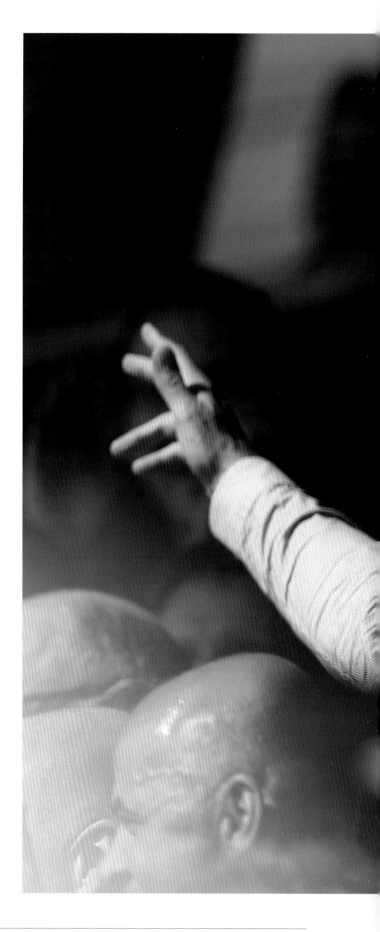

2000

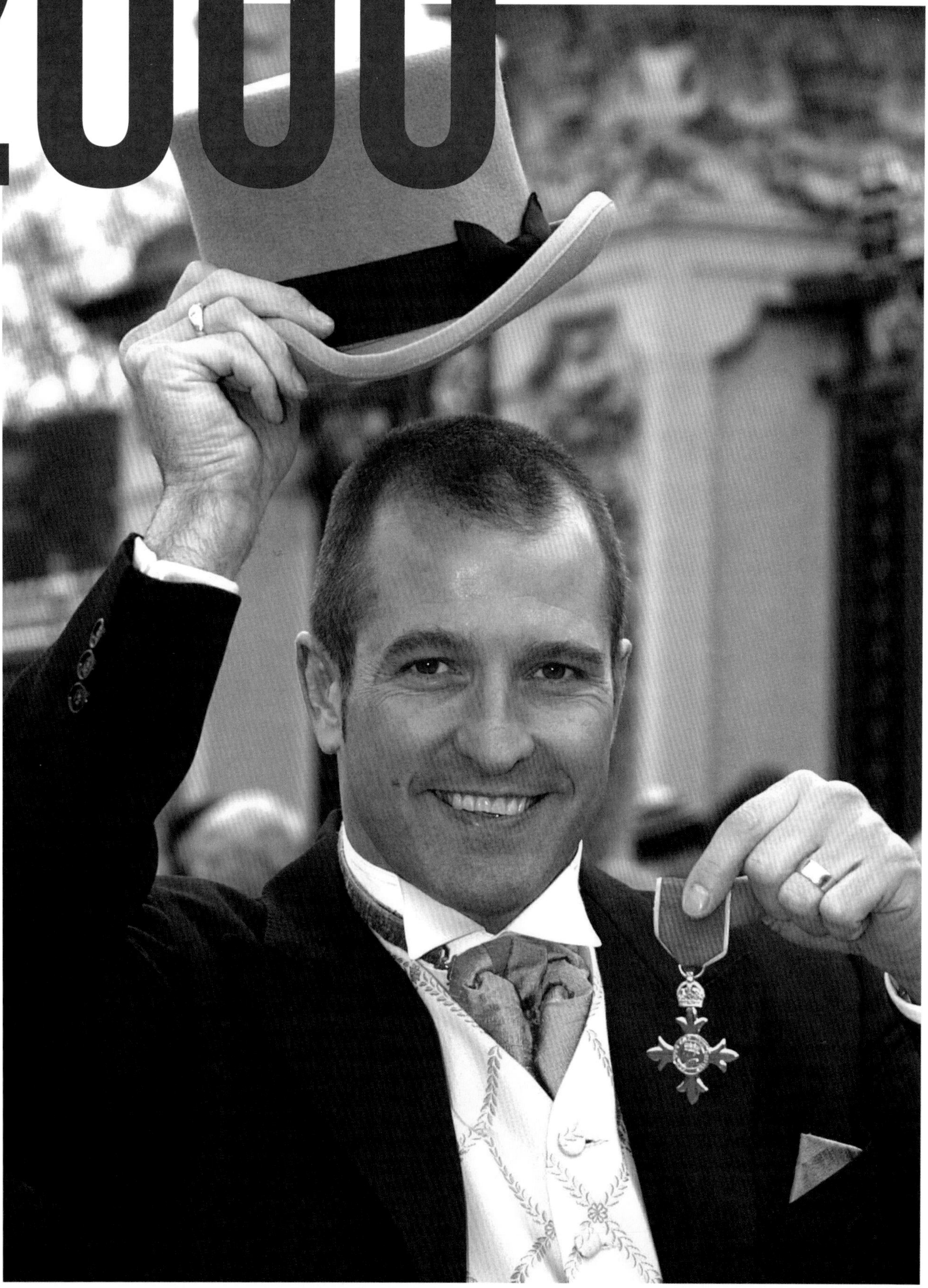

In 2000 came one of the proudest days of Bully's life as the lad from Tipton travelled to Buckingham Palace to collect an MBE from the Queen.

"You get a letter about it - which in my case came from John Major - and you can't tell people for about three months.

The problem is whenever you receive something like that and it tells you not to tell anyone, you want to tell someone don't you?

I kept it quiet and then all the details arrived about where to go for the ceremony and what will happen.

I just remember thinking 'me, getting that? What's going on?' I only played football and did some work for charity.

We went down there, with my wife at the time and my two boys and it was an unbelievable place. It was huge, the pictures on the walls were bigger than my house!

We were all given instructions about what would happen and how the ceremony would go - things like 'don't speak to the Queen until she speaks to you' and when to step forward.

There were 3,000 people there. I would have loved to have said to her 'do you get fed up of this?' Probably wouldn't have been the best thing I'd ever done – maybe next time I see her!

I remember watching on the screen as we are waiting and everyone else is going through. Sue Barker was there that day. She walked up there, bowed and must have missed the Queen's head by millimetres!

I thought if I ever did that....

Anyway, then it was 'Stephen George Bull' and, after waiting for a good while, it was my turn. I stepped forward and I tell the story now in my after dinner speech.

There is someone behind the Queen who tells her who the people are as they come forward – even the Queen can't remember that many.

As an example, they might say to her 'yes Maam, this is Stevie Bull, he's from Tipton and he's a Tatter.'

So I walked forward and bowed.

She says to me 'I have heard you played football for Wolves and scored a lot of goals.'

'Yes,' I replied. 'I absolutely loved it, scored goals for fun, loved it.'

'And you do a lot of work in and around the community as well. Very well done – keep up the good work.'

I stepped back and turned to walk away and The Queen started laughing. I stopped, turned and said 'what are you laughing at?' She replied: 'I just can't believe you actually played for the Albion.....!'

Of course it's not true, but that's the story I tell when I speak and it usually gets a good response!

In all seriousness it was a huge honour to meet the Queen and get that accolade, it was an unbelievable experience.

From playing football in front of 66,000 people at Hampden Park to meeting our lovely Queen, I have been through some fairly different experiences! It was a great experience and I absolutely loved it and will never forget it.

I wouldn't say I was particularly emotional about it. Getting a medal from the Queen – I think the feeling was more nervousness. Like when you go out of the tunnel for the first time.

It was that sort of anticipation. And then when it's over there's a big sigh of relief at the end!

I had a big top hat on, really sweaty palms and then after 18 seconds or so it's all done and dusted. An unbelievable experience."

2006

ASHBY LONDON
ACCIDENT REPAIR SPECIALISTS
INSUHEAT
AutoScan QA
Norton Bathrooms
CHEVROLET
mazda
MAZDA
Prime Time
Express & Star

"It was great to mark my 20th anniversary year and great that Wolves gave me that benefit game against Aston Villa – Mick McCarthy allowed me to start the game.

I hadn't been on a pitch for a while before that, but I'd tried to keep myself in shape and I wanted to get 20 minutes or so and give it my best. Hey – maybe if I'd scored Mick would have signed me up!

But when I was stretching to warm up I heard my knee pop again. A piece of bone had broken off the inside again. Gutted! If you look at the ten minutes I was on the pitch I was running with a bent leg. The ball came over the top to me at one point, if I'd have been able to bring it under control I might have scored. Can you imagine!

It wasn't to be and that was it for me and I've not really been able to play any charity games since."

2008

After retirement it always seemed a logical step that Bully would move into management.

A brief spell coaching at Hereford United with Graham Turner followed immediately after his Wolves playing career (including a final few cameo appearances).

But it wasn't until 2008 that Bully took the plunge and landed his first manager's job with non-league Stafford Rangers.

"It was always in my head to consider management. As I came to the end of my career I was thinking about it and whether I should have a go.

I went through a divorce and put my coaching books up in the loft. I was halfway through my 'A' license but the books went up and I haven't really picked it up since.

I tried with Stafford Rangers and had 10 months there. There were some great people there, great players and I loved it. It was just that the board wanted success straightaway and that was always going to be difficult so they pulled the rug from under my feet.

I thought if I had stopped there for two or three years maybe that would have given me the grounding and one day I could have ended up here at Wolves.

I applied for a few jobs – Kidderminster Harriers, Telford and a few more – and nothing came of it. I sent my CV off to a lot of clubs when there were vacancies and didn't get many replies! At the time I backed off after not getting anywhere but maybe I should have pushed it further.

So there is some regret I didn't push myself but that is the way I am built. Instead I moved on to other things at the time.

I just thought 'leave it Steve – it's not going to happen' and while it wasn't something I needed to do it is always at the back of my mind because it is something that I want to do.

You can't explain what you miss about football and the dressing room unless you have been through it.

As a manager I was very much like I was as a player – what you see is what you get. It was the old fashioned style.

If players needed an arm around the shoulder I would do that – if I felt they needed a bit of a rollocking I would do that. I felt I had good man management skills.

I had worked my way up as a player and think I could have passed that on whether that was as a manager or as a number two."

Of course it was always - and indeed, remains - Bully's dream to manage Wolves. He's never been shy about admitting it. And indeed, as he reveals here, there have been two occasions when if things had gone differently he would have landed the ultimate job.

Bully hasn't ruled out a return to managment or coaching. But you get the impression there's only one club he'd want to work for...

"There was one time I got close to maybe coming in at Wolves. John Gregory was in for the job and I knew John.

He rang me up and said he wanted me to come in as his number two and learn the ropes and then when he moved on I'd be in a position to take over.

I was up for that, all day long! But I don't think John even got an interview. And so I just thought it wasn't meant to be."

And then in 2012.....

"It was after Mick McCarthy left and I phoned Steve Morgan. I think it was quarter-to-12 at night and I was on the phone to him for 45 minutes.

I just said 'give me the last 13 games' and if we stay up, I'm a winner and you're a winner. I felt it was a similar situation to when Alan Shearer went in at Newcastle, but I believed I'd have given it my best shot.

We had a good chat, but after the 45 minutes Steve said he apologised for wasting my time but he had already decided that he was going to give the job to Terry Connor.

I was just after a chance, for those 13 games, but when it didn't happen I just wanted to wish Terry all the best and to see if he could keep us up.

Unfortunately he couldn't, but there are no hard feelings from me – I just wanted to give it a go."

"I don't know what will happen now and if I will ever get back into coaching.

I love the media side of it – love doing the columns in the Express & Star and the radio stuff when I get asked.

I would love to get involved on the pitch again. But if it doesn't come I will still carry on doing what I'm doing and talking about football which I love doing even now!

If anything ever came up at Wolves, I would still jump at the chance. I would love to be part of the backroom set-up, to be in and around the dressing room.

Whether it is as a striker coach, or just someone to be like a mentor around the place, helping to give the players a push from time to time.

I would jump at the chance to pass on my experience from all the highs and lows I went through during my career.

The club know where I am if ever they need me."

Bully played for four managers during his Wolves career and here he gives his take on the job they did at Molineux.

GRAHAM TURNER

"He was a great man manager. He knew when to shout, he knew when to put his arm around your shoulder, we just got on with it.

He'll say the same, that was the best time he had in football too, from 1986 to 1992, the best team and squad.

He'd have a laugh with the players too until he knew we'd overstepped the mark and then you could look out.

It was very rare he'd come out with us. Maybe abroad, if we'd been there a week, he'd come out on the last night.

After that first 1986/87 season when we lost in the play-offs the gaffer said we couldn't have done any more than we did that year and he strengthened the squad that summer and we kicked on.

People like Mark Venus and Ally Robertson came in. It just shows how good Graham Turner was at bringing in the players that the team needed."

GRAHAM TAYLOR

"I thought Graham Taylor was a very good manager and if he'd been given the time he would have got us up.

I think the fans probably had had enough by that stage in the same way that it happened with Dave Jones and Mick McCarthy.

They felt he couldn't take us any further. But there was so much Graham did behind the scenes including getting the academy going and all those ideas off the ground. I think he would have followed all of his plans through and got us into the Premier League. I never had any sort of falling out with Graham.

When the club tried to sell me once, he said it wasn't him trying to do it – it was the people above.

And at that time I didn't want to move – I wanted to stop and carry on scoring goals for Wolves.

He was far more tactical than other managers at that time. That is no disrespect to other managers I played for but he had different methods and ways of playing and was very detailed. Him and Steve Harrison were a great duo.

Steve would be in doing the training sessions really well and working us very hard but also having a laugh and a joke at the right time.

And Graham would be there with all the tactical knowledge about the way we played and positioning and they were a good combination who worked really well together."

MARK McGHEE

Mark McGhee was good as well - he came in with Colin Lee and Mick Hickman and they did a good job.

The only thing was that sometimes he used to wind up the opposition with things that he said in the media.

I think sometimes it is better to keep quiet about things until you have done it and then you can shout it from the rooftops!

Mark McGhee never did that. Whether it was the psychology to get his own players behind him and create that siege mentality I'm not sure."

COLIN LEE

Colin Lee was a great coach. As a manager I'm not sure whether he would have made it with Wolves but as a coach he was right up there, all day long.

He respected the players and earned the respect of the players.

He would put his arm around some, dish out rollockings to others, but I think he was spot on."

2009

Standing in the Hall of Fame.....

"

"It was unbelievable to get the call to go into the first Hall of Fame at Wolves. It was the same as when I was honoured at the Wolverhampton Sons and Daughters event.

It is a great feeling to be honoured by the club or by the city for something you have done. That was a great night at the Hall of Fame dinner, back in 2009.

They gave me the famous red book which took me through from when I was born to where I was then and my old mate Thommo came on stage to talk about the good old days!

I was inducted on the same night as some real Wolves legends such as Stan Cullis, Billy Wright, Ron Flowers and Derek Parkin. To be up there with those names and all that have followed, is a very humbling experience.

I feel privileged to be a part of it and there is now a section in the Wolves Museum which is devoted to the Hall of Fame."

Attending Wolves games aside, how else does Bully spend his 'retirement'? Not, it is fair to say, with his slippers and pipe, sat in front of the fire!

As detailed elsewhere in this publication, he remains heavily involved in charity activities and has plenty of close friends and family with whom he enjoys an active social life.

But he has also been involved in several different business ventures, many of which are also ongoing.

"When it became clear that the management or coaching route wasn't really going to happen, then I started to look into different things.

I have been involved in a restaurant called Bravaccio's (Bully's in Italian) in Tettenhall for a few years.

I used to go in there as a player and loved the place. When me and Terry Bolus took on the lease, we gutted the place from top to bottom and gave it a whole new look.

We were very 'hands on' - t-shirt and shorts on, knocking walls down, ripping fireplaces out, the lot!

My wife Kirsty and her business partner Jacky have a very successful events company – Steve Bull Events.

Kirst and Jack organise loads of events throughout the year including golf days, dinners, private parties etc. I host all of the events for them and help out wherever I can.

We have worked alongside lots of great people over the years, some of whom you can see above.

I also do after dinner speaking and personal appearances at weddings, birthday parties and so on.

And of course there is my charity work which I love - I think this has to be the most rewarding..."

And having a chat is something that comes far more easily to Bully now than perhaps it did as a player.

He readily admits that he always used to prefer to do his talking on the pitch, rather than in front of the microphones.

Now though he is an accomplished event host and after dinner speaker, delivering his lines with impressive timing and a ready chunk of good old-fashioned Black Country humour.

He is also no longer as nervous as he used to be.

"When I was interviewed when I was playing I think my answers were always just 'yes' or 'no'. That's all it was," he says. Yes, no, yes, no. Unbelievable!

But when I finished, my financial advisor Phil Oaten, who has looked after my finances for 30 years, told me I should get on the speaking circuit.

He said I'd be fine.

I said I couldn't do that, I couldn't tell stories, keep conversations going for that long - it wasn't what I was used to. He persisted and told me to do it so I thought I'd try.

I got a few stories together and practised them all in the front room in front of a mirror!

The first few were very nerve-racking. I was thinking before I went on, 'what am I doing'? I was so nervous. Shaking.

I wouldn't sleep the night before. But people told me I wasn't up there to try and be funny, I was up there to tell people stories and they wanted to listen.

I still get nervous now, but am far happier and more comfortable than I used to be.

It's water off a duck's back to be fair. I'm nervous at the start but once I get going I'm fine and I really enjoy it.

It is quite hard to speak for 45 minutes but I have got used to it!"

Retirement? Nah. Bully is now busier than ever!

The football now is, however, restricted to a few kickabouts with daughter Gracie.

Post-Wolves he did appear for Hereford and score a couple of goals, as well as representing the club in the Masters, playing in charity matches and enjoying six minutes back on the hallowed Molineux turf to mark his 20th anniversary testimonial game a decade ago.

But some of the legacies of his extensive career and bearing the brunt of defenders' tackling at a time when referees were less, shall we say, strict, have left their mark!

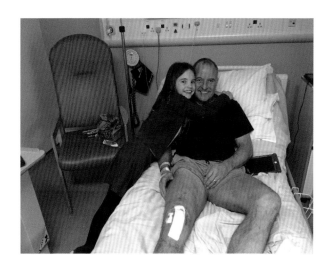

"I still get grief from my knee. Earlier this year I had two steel plates put in there to straighten it up!

Fingers crossed that will be it now. And then the other one will need doing as well at some point.

I still do a bit of coaching with young lads and young teams when I can.

But when I do that I do suffer a few days later – with everything! I still love it though.

There's a 13-year-old striker I do a bit of regular coaching with and I'm always trying to join in.

I have to remind myself to 'leave it' – otherwise I'll finish up in an even bigger mess!

My knees will be a problem for the rest of my life. But as long as I can walk, play golf, cycle, cross-train, just keep myself in decent shape, then I'll keep on doing it."

"Fitness wise I still do what I can, or at least what I am still capable of doing after all those injuries.

It did take its toll over the 13 years I played for Wolves.

The part knee replacement I had can be restrictive. But being active, keeping fit, has always been part of my life and I want that to continue.

I want to get up and go and do things and if I can get myself to the gym three days a week, four days a week, it's all good to keep the heart ticking over. I think if you can keep fit, keep that heart working, you can live a long and happy life – and I enjoy keeping myself fit.

Kirsty always says that if I've not got to the gym then I'm a bit grumpy – and she's probably right!

When I get up in the morning I don't say a great deal, I just take Gracie to school and then it's off to the gym and the chance to let off some steam – I love it."

So yes, Bully is always going to keep busy, with charity and commercial work alongside an ever hectic family and social life. He certainly isn't going to do 'shy and retiring'..............

A MATCHDAY IN THE LIFE OF BULLY...

Bully is still very much in demand at Molineux on a matchday - whether it's meeting fans, corporate supporters or making pitchside appearances, his popularity has continued since his days as a player came to an end.

So whilst unfortunately he is no longer arriving at the players' entrance, going through to the dressing rooms and putting his kit on ready to score another goal or two, supporters are still likely to catch up with Bully somewhere around the stadium at every home game.

Here the man himself takes us through what his matchdays now involve.....

1.10pm Arrive at Molineux. As vice president I have a parking space in the Directors car park, so it's a case of parking up and walking into the main reception on Waterloo Road. Here I will often get asked for photos and autographs. It's always great to catch up with the fans and have a quick chat.

1.20pm Head to the main reception, I often bump into Graham Hughes, who was there the day I signed 30 years ago. Graham is a real Wolves legend if ever there was one. See if there is any post for me on reception - can't believe I still get fan mail after all these years!

1.30pm Chat to the commercial team and find out who they want me to meet today. Usually a list of different supporters or companies in the various hospitality areas. It is always good to work with the commercial team at Wolves whether it's on a matchday or at golf days and other events.

1.40pm: Start my 'rounds', meeting all the different people. As I have said many times, I can't believe the fans still want to speak to me after all these years. But it is something I really appreciate and I am always happy to chat and have pictures taken. I have got to know a lot of Wolves supporters down the years. Many have gone on to become good friends as well.

Sometimes I will be asked to speak in the hospitality lounges either in the Billy Wright Stand or over in WV1. One of the staff from Wolves will ask me some questions and ask me to predict the score. Always a Wolves win of course! Then some more photos and chats with the guests after I have finished speaking. I used to hate standing up and speaking in front of people. As you might remember from my interviews as a player I never said a great deal! It is far more natural for me now though and I enjoy doing it and having some banter with the interviewer.

2.55: Back through the lounges to get ready to watch the game. Unless I've been asked to sit somewhere specific or go into WV1, I tend to stand just on the steps above the tunnel. It's like my Season Ticket space! You get a great view from there but you are also really involved with being able to hear the reactions of the crowd. I'd still rather be down there walking out of the tunnel with the players and getting ready for that first whistle. But unfortunately that couldn't go on for ever - and watching is the best alternative! It's great now too that Gracie wants to come to the games as well. She's got the kit and everything!

3.45: Half Time. Chance for a bit of a breather
And to update my official Facebook page
– facebook.com/bullybully9wwfc

I only launched my Facebook fans page recently as I approached the 30th anniversary. Thanks a lot for following, it is much appreciated. I laugh at some of the comments you lot post - and the dodgy photos!

4.50: Having watched the second half then comes the end of the game and hopefully a decent result for Wolves. Time to wander back and out through reception and in the car for home. Obviously it's nothing like the buzz of playing, but you can't beat a matchday at Molineux. Especially when the team win!

FAMILY LIFE

From growing up on the streets of Tipton with parents George and Joan, four sisters and one brother, to life at home now with wife Kirsty and their nine-year-old daughter Gracie Jo, family has always been hugely important.

At home, in his early years, Bully remembers the Bull family didn't have much. Certainly no luxuries. But they had enough. Mum and Dad did everything they could to provide for their children. No doubt hard work, determination, togetherness, even 'team spirit' were the order of the day.

Familiar qualities to those who were to watch the man play his football in later years.

"I had a great upbringing, I couldn't have asked for any more. Yes it was in what people might call a 'rough' area and we didn't have much money, but we just got on with it.

I think that went a long way to making me who I am – if I'd been brought up in a different situation, in a posh suburb with a load of money, it could have been different.

I was brought up in a good way, the right way, to look after everything you had and make the very most of it. It was a bit rough, coming from Tipton we had to scrimp and scrape.

My Mom had a day job working long hours in a factory called Connex Sanbra. Mom also took a second job where she would count pins into boxes on an evening to ensure we had enough money to provide us with everything we needed.

But it was a great life, I loved it and wouldn't change it for anything. I still pop back to Tipton now and again and see where I lived, where I used to kick a ball against the wall and I will bump into my mates from time to time."

There was for the young Bull, like so many of his ilk at a young age, the desire to kick a ball as much as was humanly possible. Even if that spelled a bit of bother when it came to not exactly getting properly kitted out!

"I'd come back from school with my school gear and shoes on, dump my bag and then go straight off and kick a ball around the park. I'd come back with scuffed shoes and muddy clothes and would then get a clip around the earhole from Mom!

I remember when she bought me my first pair of football boots – Dalglish Puma Kings. So yes, I was into football from a very early age.

People still ask me now who I support and I grew up as a strong Liverpool fan. There was no way we could ever afford to get to a Liverpool game, I was an armchair supporter.

They were always on the telly and I always watched and thought that I wanted to be like Ian Rush."

All those hours kicking the ball around and those strong family values, were to combine to provide the catalyst for Bully to go on and forge such a successful career in the game. And without fail, wherever he went, his two biggest supporters would be there. Mum and Dad. Bully smiles.

"They would follow me absolutely everywhere. Wherever I played, they would be up there in the stands, watching, supporting and doing plenty of cheering!.

They used to have the front two seats kept for them on the Supporters Coach with Muriel and Albert Bates and travelled to every away game with their home-made sandwiches in a Mother's Pride bag!

My Mom has sadly passed away now and my Dad doesn't go to the Wolves anymore.

But I still take him programmes from the matches and he still asks me how the team are doing.

He gives his opinions that's for sure! Maybe that is where I get some of my straight-talking from!

All the way through, he has treated me the same as he ever did. I'm not Steve Bull the footballer. I am just his son. 'Our Ste'. Full stop. And that is how it should be."

The loss of Bully's Mum Joan three years ago hit him hard, as it would anyone.

She was a lively and engaging character and the sense of pride in all of her children shone through. She was very much the driving force of the family. Known as Mrs Bull. To such an extent that Bully's wife Kirsty still finds it difficult when she is called Mrs Bull. As Kirsty says: 'There is only one Mrs Bull!"

That pride in 'Our Ste' was never more pronounced than when the man himself just happened to score his first goal for England. It came against Scotland at Hampden Park, in front of a crowd of 63, 282 on his international debut, with him having come on as a substitute.

It was a goal that produced a range of ecstatic reactions from all of a gold and black persuasion whether up there in Scotland or watching on the television at home. As were an immensely proud Mr and Mrs Bull.

"Mom and Dad were watching the game at home. This was long before mobiles, so I managed to find a phone to ring up after the game.

Mom answered and said: 'your father's not very happy'.

'Why?' I replied. I had just scored my first goal for England after all! "Well," Mum said. "I was sitting in front of the telly with a bowl on my lap scraping some potatoes – and then you scored. I jumped up and the potatoes went everywhere! Your Dad's got no tea.......good goal though son!"

As mentioned earlier it is a fairly big family that Bully is a part of. Again, like many families, they may not meet up as much as they would all like. But, in times of trouble, they each know where they are!

"I've got four sisters and one brother, a big family! We all get on. Maybe we don't see each other as much as we should – probably like a lot of families – but we all know we are on the end of the phone whenever it is needed.

I love each and every one of them to bits and when we do get together we just pick up from where we left off and have a great time.

Families to me are like ex-players. They have got their own lives, but you know where they are when you need them.

You don't live in each other's pockets and you meet up now and again, but you know you are always there for each other.

To them I think I am just their brother, they know I'm no different to anyone else."

Family life for Bully has been extended further over the last decade-and-a-bit. In 2004, Bully, who already had two sons, Jack and Joe from his previous marriage, married wife Kirsty. The two are partners not only in life but also in work, with Kirsty running Steve Bull Events with close friend Jacky Carr as well as the charitable Steve Bull Foundation.

There remains plenty of time for family life as well and it is fair to say that plenty of that is needed to keep Gracie entertained!

Whether it be on the school run, trips to the cinema, or even having to sit down and watch the odd reality TV show, Bully loves doing his bit!

"We have been blessed with Gracie coming along as a daughter for myself and Kirsty. It took a bit of time, we went through IVF and on the third time we struck gold. Another hat trick eh? Maybe that was my 19th!!!

Nine months later Kirsty gave birth to Gracie - we were so fortunate and Gracie is absolutely brilliant.

She keeps me young, she keeps me vibrant. I will take her anywhere and do anything for her.

I love doing the school run and am very fortunate that I can do that on a daily basis. Gracie is also becoming a bit of a Wolves fan now.

She's got the kit and comes along to the games with me now by my side! She's fantastic and I wouldn't change her for the world."

"She has already said what she wants to do when she is older – help her Mum with organising events!

Kirsty will take her to work with her as well and she will get cracking on the computer which is brilliant.

She knows a lot more than me, she sorts everything out with my phone and so on – kids and technology is frightening isn't it?

Kirsty has been great for me as well. She probably won't like me for saying this, but she is like the engine to my car!

She guides me and pushes me in the right direction.

Her events company, Steve Bull Events, is brilliant, Kirst and Jacky really look after people properly. (And me!)

I think we both respect each other, absolutely and you have to have that in a relationship.

We have our time as a family and we have our own time and that is the way it should be.

What do we do if we are at home together? The two of them gang up on me!

They want to watch Emmerdale or Coronation Street, or some reality show or another.

When that happens I'm usually off up to Gracie's room where I stick Sky on and watch the football instead!

It's all good though and we do the normal stuff that families enjoy.

We've got a trampoline in the garden and Gracie gets the football out as well, it is normal day-to-day stuff that families do and I really enjoy it.

It is not always smooth, course it's not, I'm not sure any family has it always smooth. We all have our ups and downs, like anyone, but we deal with them together."

One day, of course, will come the time when there will be a knock at the door and Gracie will be off out on a date, with someone, to somewhere.

Every Dad's nightmare? To see their Princess heading into that territory?

(Bully laughs) "It is what it is.

When that day arrives I'll be upstairs with a catapult ready to take him out!

No, seriously, I am sure I will have a quiet chat and say that if Gracie comes home crying don't come back again!

Ha ha, only joking. She is great and as a Dad you will always want to look after her.

That's the way it works isn't it?"

Indeed it is and from Tipton to Compton and a few other locations in between, Bully is clearly now happy and content and enjoying everything that family life has to offer.

And now a few words from Gracie...

MY DAD

I like it when me and Daddy go out on our bikes. And when we play football in the back garden or in the street.

We also go out together for walks with our dog Bessie.

Once when I lost my favourite hair clip Dad took me everywhere to try and find it. But we never did.

Sometimes when my Mom says that I can't have something, I will go and see Dad. And if he is in a good mood he will let me have it! Then Mom goes mad.

When my Mom is away or out with her friends we will watch movies together.

We watched Cloudy with a Chance of Meatballs and we were both just laughing all the time.

The little monkey on there just keeps going "Steeeeeeve". And we both kept laughing!

My Mom says we are like two peas in a pod.

I come to the Wolves matches with Dad now which is nice. I like to wear the Wolves kit.

When I walk with him we have to stop all the time for him to sign autographs or have pictures.

I think the Wolves fans love him a lot.

It takes us ageeeeees to get inside!

I saw his name on the stand once and I said to him: "Of all the people in all the world, why did they pick you to have your name on that stand?"

He said: "I don't know," and I said: "Why couldn't they pick another footballer?"

I know that he is famous at Wolves and it is nice that he is my Dad.

If I had to pick a day out with my Dad, we would go to the cinema to watch a funny film and then go to Mackies (McDonalds). We love Mackies.

I like going to the racing too with Dad and to see all the horses, Dad loves the races.

Sometimes me and Mom will be watching the TV and he will want to watch the footy and I will say: "That's not even your team."

And I will say: "Well we want to watch our programmes Dad."

So he goes into my playroom and watches football in there - he doesn't mind though.

Once I was in my playroom to watch a movie and he was hiding behind the door. He jumped out and scared me and he made me cry! I think my Dad has a brain the size of a walnut.

But I am very proud of him and very happy that he is my Dad and I love him.

Gracie Jo Bull, aged 9.
November, 2016.

Here's what Kirsty has to say...

MY HUSBAND

I first met Steve in 1993 when I was 20 and I worked on reception at Wolves. I was not a Wolves fan but I knew who he was.

My brother Nick had posters of Steve on his wall when he was younger and I remember Nick and my Dad going to a big football game at Wembley to see their beloved team play in the Sherpa Van Final.

To me he was just Steve, same as all the other players who came in and out of the club on a daily basis. They were a very down to earth bunch of lads, they had great banter with each other, laughing and joking non stop.

You didn't often see Steve without his mate Thommo though – they went everywhere together and Steve still thinks the world of him.

We have been together 16 years, married for 12 and I have to say Steve is a great husband and an amazing Daddy to our daughter Gracie Jo.

We have a very happy life; it's a busy one, but all good. We have lovely family and friends around us, Steve often says: "We are very lucky people." I agree.

Considering we work together, we get on quite well really, he doesn't mind me telling him what to do, I don't think - as long as I don't nag him too much!

Steve gets asked to do loads of stuff and he always says : "I don't know what I'm doing mate – ask Kirst!" He doesn't own a diary.

I am very proud to say he is my husband, he is a great man with a heart as big as the club he loves, Wolverhampton Wanderers.

Kim on behalf of the Bull clan – also sisters Lilian, Lynda, Jane and brother Alan....

"

MY BROTHER

As kids we were all in it together. The girls had one bedroom and the boys had another. And Mom and Dad had another.

We weren't privileged to have a room each but we just got on with it. We all went to school and did our schoolwork and if we were naughty we'd get punished.

I asked the other girls what they wanted me to write about Steve as a boy and the general response was: "He was a little sod!'

Ste was a typical brother, as brothers are. We'd be off playing with dolls and prams and he went off playing with a ball. We had our spats like all brothers and sisters do but generally we all got on. We would all stick up for one another and our Mom was the best at that.

If anyone gave any of her kids any grief, she'd be there! We weren't naughty children, we all got on and then, as we got older, we all went our different ways. Things happen and then the circle turns and everyone comes back. As we have got older, I think we have got closer.

We are more appreciative of where we come from, how lucky we have been in relationships and home life and Steve has had all of his success.

None of us went to college or further education, we had to go out and get a job. Steve was in the right place at the right time to get his opportunity.

And he took it – yes, he took the bull by the horns! He did what he had to do to get where he has got.

People I speak to now still say he is a legend but what he did in football was what he does with everything. He gets his head down, gets on with it and gives it everything he can for a good outcome. He worked so hard for what he got. In football maybe he was a bit early, he could have been better off later on, but pound signs weren't in Steve's eyes. I don't think he wanted to move. He wanted to stay here, stay loyal and stay with the family.

He has had his ups and downs in his life, like all of us, but he has dusted himself down and carried on.

And now, with his football finished, he is doing a lot of work with his charities and in the community which I think is really commendable.

It is fabulous what he does, giving something back.

We would all follow his football closely.

My Mom used to take him off everywhere to play football when he was younger in her little yellow Robin Reliant – folded up his bike and put him in there! Mom was actually an Albion fan, but whatever team Steve played for she was going to follow them. And Dad was always there as well – they would go to all of the games, home and away.

He has stayed the same Steve all the way through. We've all stayed the same - just got older and wiser! Although I think Steve's speech has improved. That Tipton accent has got a bit better! He does hold his cards very close to his chest sometimes and can be guarded. He'll say: "Don't worry about me, just worry about you."

But then once he has had a drink or two he quickly loosens up!

When it's needed, we all rally around together like we did when Mom passed away. We are just one good family unit and while we are not in each other's pockets, we all know that anyone is just a phone call away.

When it comes to the anniversary of Mom passing we'll all go for a game of bingo because that is what she used to like doing. Half the night is spent laughing and we'll end up getting told off for making too much noise!

Ste will rib us about stuff and we'll give it him back. But he's done good hasn't he?

We are all very proud of him.

And from George...

MY SON

When our Ste was very young he used to go over the park. He'd put two jackets down – one for one goalpost and one for the other. We never had much money to spare, so Ste found an old burst case-ball which we stuffed with old newspaper – we couldn't afford a bladder. He'd be over there on his own, in all weather, kicking the ball around for hours.

I used to do a bit of work pulling pints in the pub and one Sunday dinner time, when it was pouring down with rain, this chap comes in. He asked who the kid was on the park playing football, who was wringing wet! "That'll be my young-un," I replied. "He just loves playing football."

A scout called Sid Day took him to Tipton Town. He came home one day, not happy because he said they weren't going to pick him. Sid took him back and they gave him a few matches, but it still wasn't working out, so he took him to the Albion for a trial.

There he met Johnny Giles the manager and Ste was offered £100 a week to play for the Albion. That was the same money he was getting for working 80 hours as a forklift driver. He couldn't believe it so of course he took it! I remember going down on my bike to watch them train at Spring Road.

Nobby Stiles had got our Steve and he had him running and sprinting from one end of the pitch to the other. And again. And again. When he got home he said: "Dad, he's killing me!"

But Nobby had told him he didn't want any pretty football from him – he wanted the effort and the goals. Nobby Stiles was the best bloke. Steve scored a few goals for Albion and then, the one day, I was doing some bricklaying at a church in Hill Top and Bully and Thommo arrived.

November 20th, 1986. I remember the date even now. 'What are yow doing?' I said. And they told me Ron Saunders had sold them both! He'd got them both in and told them they were both going to Wolves.

It all took off from there. Steve and Andy Mutch were the best two strikers you could ever meet. They were telepathic. They each knew what the other one was doing and Wolves got so many goals as a result.

Myself and my wife Joan never missed a match, home or away, for ten years. We'd watch him everywhere. We'd work our holidays so we could get the time off on a Saturday and travel on the supporters' coach to go and watch him play. I never got nervous watching him, not like Joan, oh apart from once. The time he went up for the header against Villa and Spink and McGrath came in and he was left on the floor. The ball still ended up in the net even then!

We were at home watching on telly when he got his first England cap, coming off the bench against Scotland. Gary Stevens knocked the ball in, it hit his shoulder, he turned and bang. In the back of the net. We jumped up and everyone came out of their houses into the street. It was great. We didn't go to the World Cup though, we watched that at home. But we went to all the games he played at Wembley, including the Czechoslovakia game when he scored twice – that Gazza made both of them. I've got the video tape in there of almost all of his goals. But I can't watch them anymore – there's no video on the telly! But I can still remember most of them. I've got them all up here in my head.

I never thought that my lad would go from kicking a ball in the rain on the park to playing for England at a World Cup. Nobody would, would they? Nobody would. He just had it in him, he wanted to be a footballer. He had the right attitude and that took him all the way.

Me and Joan were always very proud of him, of what he has done with his life. But we didn't take too much notice of everything else that went with it. We weren't any different to any other parents and Steve didn't change after what happened to him.

We were proud of all of our children, whatever they did in life. We were a close family.

WHAT THE FANS SAY...

From surprising fans at weddings, to reducing grown men to tears, Bully has always had an effect on those fans who follow him and indeed adore him. Here are just a few of the thousands of memories of those Wolves supporters who took Bully to their hearts.

It was back in October, 2013, when I had to miss the Coventry game to attend my stepdaughter Sarah and Jono's fantastic wedding.

This story went viral because it was to be my only missed game at Molineux in then, 37 years and now over 40 years. Many stories and pictures appeared in national and local newspapers and online plus there were lots of radio interviews and that day the news was the number one read article online on the BBC.

This was made all of the more spectacularly memorable by one of my all-time Wolves favourite players, the incredible Steve Bull – 306 goal hero for Wolves – unbelievably arriving at the wedding reception having travelled down to Suffolk to surprise me. One of the most incredible moments of my Wolves supporting life.

This again went viral with more stories, pics and radio interviews the following week plus Wolves then arranging for Bully and Thommo to present me, pitchside at Molineux, with a superb framed picture at the Oldham game the following Tuesday.

Fantastic memories and the biggest thank you of all to the amazing Bully – happy 30th at the Mol.

PETER ABBOTT

I've witnessed many of Bully's 306 Wolves goals. His goalscoring exploits with his numerous hat-tricks, local derby goals and last minute winners are many of my fondest footballing memories. But one recollection of Bully's playing career and his bond between the Molineux faithful that stands out in my memory is from a reserve fixture back in 1999.

On a cold March evening whilst most football supporters would have preferred to stay at home and watch a night of Champions League football on the TV. Wolves reserves played host to Bolton Wanderers reserves. For Steve Bull it was his first comeback game after a knee injury which had ruled him out for several months. The crowd for such a fixture would have normally been a few hundred at best, but on that night and with the Billy Wright stand nearing capacity as the kick-off approached, Wolves officials had to open the Stan Cullis stand to cater for the thousands of supporters that had turned up. A crowd of over 8,000 were present to see their idol return. I remember when the team ran out on the pitch and with the sight of Bully amongst the starting line-up a massive cheer went up, Bully turned, smiled and acknowledged the crowd. The pride on his face was a picture as he knew every one of those supporters were there solely to see their hero return to competitive action.

Whilst the faces change in football there are a few players that stand out above the crowd and live long in supporters' memories. Steve Bull is certainly one of those. I'd just like to thank Steve Bull for all the goals and great memories.

TIM GIBBONS

I remember when Bully came to the Wolves. I loved the way that he played and I would travel from Reading just to see him play. I just knew he would play for England from early on in his career. I started to get my head shaved and even took the nickname of Bully, which I still have!

MARK 'BULLY' CANNON

Steve Bull has always been my hero! I've met him hundreds of times and every time he goes out of his way, even just to say hello. I once got him to sign my leg and went to have it tattooed there and then! He called me crazy but at least now I'll forever have a piece of my hero with me. I remember the day he hung up his boots - I cried my heart out...for about a week!

LUCY GREATREX

A colossus, watching him reeling away, arms outstretched like an aeroplane, after dispatching another hat trick is truly one of the greatest moments I have experienced as a Wolves fan. The Molineux terraces when I was a young lad had been in such decay - it was a really dark period in our clubs existence. Bully put all the heartache and misery, our great club's free-fall created, firmly behind us as we regained pride and passion in the old gold and black.

He really is one of our own - A true Black Country Legend.

IAN 'DICKIE' DAVIES

I will forever be in Bully's debt for the simple reason that I remained a single man throughout his career with us. Without regret I once said to a girlfriend with an itchy family that I could never get married whilst Bully was wearing a Wolves shirt, as I was following him up and down the country and it wouldn't be fair. When the papers said he was on the verge of leaving for Coventry, it was squeaky bum time.

As it turns out Bully's Wolves career extended further than said girlfriend. On reflection I think I had happier days watching him plunder so many more goals for us, than anything else at that time.

DAVID MARTIN

My dad and I watched Bully in his first England game against Scotland. When he scored my Dad jumped up out of his seat and punched the air. However he punched the glass light above him smashing it. When it fell it landed in the glass coffee table. Fantastic to see his first goal but it ended up costing my Dad £400!

TONY BROOKES

I've managed to meet, or at least say hi, on a few occasions but the one that sticks out the most was on 11 April, 1990. Bully was doing a meet the fans and Q&A session at the Goldthorn Social Club near Fighting Cocks.

The event went well but I remember the young Steve Bull being just as interested to get into the back room and watch the FA Cup semi final replay between Man Utd and Oldham and have a pint as the Q&A itself, which went down well with many other fans there too.

Two months later he was playing for England at the World Cup so it was a memorable time. He signed my old Manders shirt, which has never been washed since and is just about hanging in there with other memorabilia!

Living abroad now I don't get to many games but glad to hear after 30 years he is still part of the furniture - congratulations.

MATT LEVETT

I count myself lucky to have been present at both the 1974 and 1980 League Cup Finals and watching a Wolves team boasting the likes of Richards, Dougan, Bailey, Hibbitt, Munro etc. A young lad of just 19, I remember thinking on the way back from Wembley having just beaten Brian Clough's European Champions that life as a Wolves fan couldn't get any better!

Initially I was spot on. In fact it deteriorated so quickly that just six years after beating Nottingham Forest and lifting the trophy for the second time in a similar period, Wolves suffered consecutive relegations and found themselves in the Fourth Division.

Even worse the ground was falling apart, crowds were dropping to an all time low and the club faced the very real possibility of going under. A founder member of the football league and one of the most famous names in European football were on their knees crying out for a saviour...... When Stephen George Bull signed for an initial fee of £54.000, it was seen as something of a gamble. A young, raw, hard working local centre forward with a poor first touch - surely this man would not turn out to be the saviour we were all praying for?

Being totally honest I remember very little about his debut. In fact his first three games were less than memorable and I certainly didn't see anything that made me think we were about to witness one of the great footballing stories. That all changed on a Tuesday night in Cardiff, his first goal in the old gold led to another and another, eventually breaking record after record and a journey that had started at Tipton Town in 1984 culminated in World Cup Final appearances for England in Italia 1990.

The man was not just a saviour - for many of us he was like a GOD. The 18 hat tricks, 306 goals, all were memorable but two games in particular will always be my favourites.

15th October, 1989. West Bromwich Albion away. The scores were level at 1-1 with the time ticking away when Bully rammed home the winner at the Smethwick End where the thousands of Wolves fans were gathered. That is still the greatest feeling I have had in my 46 years following the club and I doubt many present would disagree.

The second came less than three months later, Newcastle away - January 1st, 1990. Like many others I had flown up with Hatherton Wolves. A 4-1 victory with Bully scoring every goal. I can't remember the journey back but we were on such a high we could have probably managed it without a plane.

From 1988 to 1990 I seemed to spend more time at Wembley than I did at home. Two Wolves appearances and numerous England games, Steve was living the dream and so were the thousands of fans following his every step.

Just before his Wolves career came to a sad end in the summer of 1999, I had buried my beloved nan but kept my emotions in check. A few weeks later Bully walked out at Molineux to thank the fans for their support over the years and for us to show him the respect he deserved. I cried in public that day, something I had never done before and have never repeated, Bully really was, and still is, that special.

Over recent years Steve has helped me many times with various charity events and I am proud to call him a friend. Even now, when we are talking, I still think back to the good old days when I would have travelled anywhere to watch him play. A normal down to earth bloke in so many ways but a true legend to those of us lucky enough to witness one of the greatest stories in Wolves history.

STEVE PLANT

WHAT HIS FRIENDS SAY...

Bully has been privileged to have made many close friends in his life, the majority of whom he met during his playing career or via other Wolves activities. Unfortunately we were unable to speak to all of those friends – that would be an entire book by itself – but caught up with a few to grab an anecdote or two about what Bully is like behind the scenes.

Bully with Chris and his daughter Liv

Bully with Phil

PHIL OATEN

I got to know Steve back in 1990, when I first gave him some financial advice and have become good friends with him since. I have seen his confidence improve dramatically over the years, particularly with the Q&As and public speaking which he first did during his testimonial year in 1996.

I used to take him to the Midland Sporting Club boxing and the one night there had been a raffle. There was a guy bouncing a Wolves ball he had won and Steve said: "Don't do that, it's valuable." The bloke was a Birmingham City supporter!

I went to the bar and came back a few minutes later and the two of them were deep in conversation. And the guy said: "I used to hate him, he used to flatten our goalkeeper, score goals against us all the time and I've started talking to him and he's one of nicest blokes I have ever met!" That's Steve and it's a pleasure for me to be good mates with him.

CHRIS SHARRATT

I have known Steve for about 30 years, from when he signed for Wolves, as we both lived in Norton Canes.

Initially he was shy and retiring. Never one for the limelight, but always prepared to pass the time of day with anyone.

His confidence has grown over the years, but he still has the ability to communicate at all levels and never turns away anyone who asks for a photograph with him and believe me when I say it's young and old. I remember once a girl in her late teens or early 20's came up to him and say: "Hadn't you used to be Steve Bull? My Dad loves you, can I have a photograph with you?"

Sharp as a knife. Steve replied "Of course you can and yes I'm still Steve Bull, I'm not so sure about your dad loving me." The girl replied: "Oh thanks - my Dad will be so pleased to have a photograph of us together."

What has always come through is his loyalty, both to Wolves and his friends.

He is always there for you, he never lets you down and is extremely kind and extremely trustworthy.

A man of the people - for the people. A man of the Black Country with Black Country values. These values explain why he is respected countrywide.

SURESH BAWA

I have known Steve since he helped launch the Promise Dreams charity for me 15 years ago and from there we have become good mates. He is very kind and generous with his time, not only to me but also my family.

Steve is such an unassuming guy, I'm not sure he understands all the adoration and will always ask, 'what is all the fuss about? I was only doing my job!' And he is always playing pranks.

I have often shared a room with Steve if we have gone away on trips and I am a bit OCD about creases in my clothes.

The one night I had ironed my clothes and went into the shower only to come back and find them all tied up in knots. I didn't say anything, just got the ironing board out and did them again, before leaving the room.

By the time I came back then yes, more knots. The clothes not nicely laid out, as I had left them. By now I wasn't amused. And there was a stony silence in the room before we went out for dinner.

Revenge was sweet, believe me I got my own back!

Steve is still a big kid at heart, still loves the footballing banter and the humour and we feel very lucky to play a part in his life. His love of fun, kindness and humbleness are a key part of his character.

Bully and Jim

JIM SHARMA

I first got to know Steve probably 25 years ago when he had been at Wolves for a few years. He was a private guy then – it was a time when he couldn't really go out anywhere without being mobbed.

We became good mates and I remember the year after he had finished playing we decided to go to every Wolves match, home and away.

There are so many stories from that season, going around the M25 twice when he was navigating, falling asleep in the back after he'd had a few beers – it was the season when it seemed like every long away trip – Grimsby, Crystal Palace you named it – was on a Tuesday night!

Steve is what he is, he doesn't pretend to be anything special and is a good mate.

STEVE COOPER

I first got to know Steve through Kirsty and she often refers to me as the guy who got rid of the Bully crewcut!

He came along to try a new style, to move away from his famous style and it took us three or four cuts but we got there in the end. Although as he gets a bit older I think he is ever so gradually returning back to it now!

I also once got him on the catwalk. Him and Thommo, when we did a charity fashion show for Promise Dreams.

I am not the biggest football fan, but I have ended up going to the odd game or two with him as well.

Steve is a great bloke and a great friend and he always has time for anyone, wherever he may be.

Bully with Steve and Suresh

WHAT THE PLAYERS SAY...

I came over to England in September 1985 to join Albion and Bully was there at the time.

So I pretty much knew him from day one of my football career.

Then we both ended up at Wolves, along with Thommo and Ally Rob and had some great successes on the pitch and a great team spirit off it.

Bully's record on the pitch and the number of goals that he scored is still there for all to see, but the big thing for me is that friendships last longer than the football and we have stayed in touch throughout this last 30 years.

Whenever we bump into each other it is almost like day one when we were first in the same dressing room. The friendship is as strong as it was when it was gathering momentum then.

It is always great to catch up and you still share the same jokes and chat about the old times which will hopefully be the case for many more years to come!

ROBBIE DENNISON

I already knew about Bully before I arrived at Wolves as a 15-year-old. He was a club legend and it was a massive honour for me to play alongside him when I broke into the team.

We built up a decent partnership, even though at times it was probably difficult for both of us to understand each other!

As a young player you always want to learn from the best and Bully's goalscoring record was second to none.

A few of us at the time were a little bit cheeky - myself and Matty and one or two others used to give him a bit of stick. All good natured of course.

We all had so much respect for him and just loved the banter that went on, however, we also knew that if he grabbed hold of us when we were giving him a bit of cheek we would be in trouble!

I remember one of the pre-season tours, when it got to the last night and we were allowed to go out.

A few of us hadn't really got any decent clothes left and we were chatting in Bully's room when all of a sudden he grabs this box full of Mizuno kit, which he'd been given for free and said 'Wear this if you want...'

No thanks Bully! I'm not sure that Mizuno gear would have really fitted the bill for a night out on the town!

It's a testament to him that he has maintained his association with Wolves for 30 years now – all the best ledge.

ROBBIE KEANE

Bully was such a hard worker.

When I was coming through as a young goalkeeper he was nearing the end of his career but he still worked so, so hard – he trained like he played.

When you saw Bully heading for the gym you wanted him to ask you in to join him because you knew how hard he worked and that it would really do you good.

But part of you didn't because you knew how tough it would be!!!

He loved scoring goals, even in training and he took the ball so early.

As a young keeper training with the first team it was a real lesson for me.

He took the ball so early and hit it so firmly that even if it was close to you it was still so difficult to keep out.

Off the pitch he was great. When I was a young keeper, as a YTS, I would travel with the team and I'd be the one making drinks on the bus. All the lads were great though – every Christmas they used to weigh me in with a nice tip! It was a respect thing. I was travelling and making my way in the game.

One day Bully said to me: "Cup of tea Matty, two sugars." And I don't know why but I just replied with, "who do you think you are? A legend or something!" I go off to make the drink and as soon as I have turned around, next thing he's got me in a headlock!

Stowelley had to come over to get his arm off me and say that if I could breathe I might be able to say sorry!!! I was 16 years of age and had never been squeezed like that in my life! I don't even know why I said it, I loved Bully. I think it was me being a little bit cheeky!

If Bully ever gave you a proper handshake, or squeezed your elbow. Oh wow, it hurt! He had the strongest grip I have ever known.

Anyway, for cheeking him he completely ripped my t-shirt. The only thing holding it together was the elastic around my arm. I had to get off the coach for the match with my t-shirt just hanging on and then quickly put my tracksuit top on.

Looking back, the young ones were all a bit cheeky at the time. Another time Bully and Keith Curle got into mine and Nayls' room when we weren't there and tied all our gear together. It went from the top floor of the hotel to the bottom, like one of those things when they escape from prison!

It has been great to stay in touch with Bully since he finished playing and to work with him at some charity and community events as well. He knows he can make a difference. He gives so much back to the local area and is a proper Wolves legend – and a top man as well!

MATT MURRAY

WHAT THE PLAYERS SAY...

In football, people need heroes and Steve Bull is certainly one of those. For someone to have a 30-year association with any club is very rare.

It's been fantastic that the people within the club have embraced his loyalty and that's been reciprocated. He was a tremendous player for Wolves and I don't think his goal record will ever be beaten.

And the loyalty he showed to the club is not something you see very often these days with players coming and going so frequently.

Thirty years is a fantastic achievement for him and his family, as well as everything he's done with his life, including of course his charity work.

It's been well documented what a fantastic partnership we had together. We both had some great times creating and scoring goals and winning games of football.

All the players in that Wolves team came from different backgrounds but we had a wonderful team spirit and were hungry for success - we wanted to achieve something.

As we've always said, me and Bully couldn't understand a word each other said - I think that's why we got on! It's always great to catch up with him - every time we get together we just carry on where we left off.

ANDY MUTCH

Bully had the most amazing ability to win a game by himself, he was such a unique talent. In the modern-day game he'd probably be priceless with that ability to be aggressive, be strong, to run and to finish.

He just told you where he wanted the ball and that was perfect for players like myself. Running towards the opposition goal Bully was unplayable; he could turn a bad ball into a good ball and he could turn a good ball into a perfect one. He also had a great foil in Andy Mutch which was a great partnership for him.

On top of all that he was such a good, grounded and down-to-earth lad. He helped the club from the equivalent of League 2 to the Championship, he got his international rewards and I think it will be a long time before Wolves will have another player that the fans can relate to in the same way. That really epitomises Steve's time at the club better than anything else.

PAUL COOK

It didn't matter what game Bully played in - away at Rochdale for Wolves or at Wembley for England - he'd give 100 per cent every single time. He proved to everyone what a fantastic goalscorer he was. And the fact he played for England and scored with them too showed you he could have done it in the Premier League.

Bully was one of those lads who just got on with it. I was one of the older players at the time and one of the good things about him was he did listen and he did learn - he was willing to listen to other people. His dad was lovely too and we got on ever so well. I was in the reserves at Albion with Bully and you could see how good he was. And then at Wolves we were just lucky that Albion got rid of him!

It was fantastic what he did for the club - he brought them up from the doldrums. But he was a great lad off the pitch too, part and parcel of the team and there was a great camaraderie among us all. We had a lot of giggles over the years and we've always kept in touch and had a laugh.

ALLY ROBERTSON

WHAT THE PLAYERS SAY...

Well, what can I say about Bully? For starters, to be tied to a club for 30 years in one capacity or another is a great achievement and he deserves everything he's got.

He's worked so hard, be it playing, or in the ambassador role he's had for a number of years.

We both moved to Wolves at the same time and we've been through it all together from the word go. It'll always be my club being a local lad as well and playing there for 11 years.

I can't believe it's been 30 years since it all began - it really does feel like yesterday.

The club was on its backside when we joined - the stands were closed, the takeover had just happened a few weeks before and gradually the rebuilding started on and off the pitch.

It was more difficult for me to move as I'd been at Albion from the age of 13, but the attraction for me was that it was my hometown club and all my friends were Wolves fans. In hindsight it was definitely the right decision! Me and Bully had been playing reserve team football together at Albion. We got on well but Bully was married so had other commitments and was shooting off so we didn't socialise a lot.

Then at Wolves it all started to click. Graham brought in a few players - me and Bully in November, then Robbie Dennison in March, Ally Robertson and Andy Mutch were already there - and it gelled straight away. With the Bull and Mutch partnership being so prolific, the rest was history.

They were great days. It was a very close knit group - it wasn't just the odd few who were mates, it was everyone. As a team and a squad we stayed together, we had a drink on a Tuesday after training and we've got some great memories of that time.

Bully obviously made a lot of the headlines with his goalscoring record but he wasn't big headed.

In fact he was anything but.

He stayed level-headed and just got on with his job. Even when he went off with England for the World Cup in 1990 we'd still get the odd phonecall off him saying he was bored!

I played with some really good players, but Bully was the best. He was totally committed and focused on what he wanted.

Some strikers, once they've scored they might think that's enough, but Bully wanted more and more. He had that drive.

He was the same in training - he gave as much effort then as he did in matches.

He always put himself about and he loved the physical side of it. He gave it out and took it, that's what made him unique.

For the first two or three years in particular when Bully and Mutchy were scoring for fun you just thought, well teams are going to have to outscore us to beat us. We had threats from all over the park as well in Dennison and Micky Holmes.

We just knew we'd score and you know what Bully's like, he created a lot of chances for himself, he didn't just need a supply line.

Me and Bully are still mates today - he's a great lad and I've always got on with him - I was even Best Man at his wedding to Kirsty.

He's always got time for others, he puts so much effort in and he's very generous.

His charity work, starting with Promise Dreams and the things he's done with his own foundation, just show what kind of bloke he is.

ANDY THOMPSON

Our paths first crossed on the football pitch. I was scoring goals for Albion in the late 1980s, while Bully was banging in 50 a season.

Albion versus Wolves then became a Second Division fixture and that was when I got to know him.

We were the two goalscorers of the teams and the Express & Star got us together for a photoshoot ahead of a Valentine's Day match at Molineux and dressed us up as gangsters, back-to-back with machine guns and pinstripe suits.

We hit it off straight away - there was a mutual respect between us.

When I joined Wolves in 1994 I came into the dressing room and he immediately nicknamed me Prince (after the pop star, not Prince Charles).

My peg was next to his in the dressing room so we had a lot of banter on a daily basis.

Put simply, it was a joy to play with him. For a lot of my career, and I say this with the greatest of respect, my game was about working hard, chasing lost causes etc, but I'd never really played alongside someone that did the same thing.

Me and Steve shared similar values and the only difference was he found the net on a much more regular basis.

We made sure that if we weren't playing well we still made it damn difficult for defenders to be comfortable. That was refreshing. I remember the time we drew 1-1 at Spurs in an FA Cup fourth round game - I managed to score and afterwards read Gary Mabbutt, who was a Premier League centre half, say it was the hardest game he and his centre half partner had all season.

He had as big a heart as you could ever wish to find and it goes without saying to score 306 goals for one club, or even in your whole career, is just the most amazing achievement.

It's testament to him that the fans still sing his name at Molineux to this day. I was at the Norwich game recently and they did exactly that - it's brilliant to hear. We've stayed great friends ever since our playing days and I see a lot of him.

I try and keep up with him when he's drinking his white wine, although that's a difficult task!

He's kind, he'll do anything for everybody. Everyone knows what he's done with Promise Dreams and his foundation. He's got the heart of a lion - he showed that on the pitch and he's showed it off the pitch too.

He's intrinsically linked with Wolves and always will be. He stayed loyal to Wolves and I'm confident the supporters and the club had an awful lot to do with that in how they identified with him. throughout his playing career and afterwards.

He's still at every home game and it still hurts him when Wolves lose.

If you cut him he'll bleed gold and black.

DON GOODMAN

During the last 30 years, there have been many column inches and plenty of broadcast space devoted to Wolves' record goalscorer. Many among the media and fanzine world who have followed his fortunes so closely are also Wolves fans themselves – a real labour of love. We asked a few for their thoughts.

WHAT THE MEDIA SAYS...

DAVID HARRISON

As someone born and raised in Tipton and a lifetime Wolves fan, I feel genuinely entitled and proud to hail Steve Bull as "one of our own."

I first became aware of my fellow Black Countryman when he was scoring goals for Tipton Town and my interest increased when he signed professionally for a club not far away from us down the A41.

I was delighted when the Tiptonian saw sense and agreed to join Wolves 30 years ago and so began a love affair between me and other Wolves supporters with a striker whose contribution and loyalty will forever remain etched in club folklore.

I got to know Bully over the years and grew to admire that down-to-earth, no-nonsense, in-your-face style, on and off the pitch, which brought him a club record number of goals and the devotion of a legion of admiring fans.

Steve and I spoke the same language and that was to prove useful when his fame spread onto the international stage.

On one of his early call-ups for England, as was normal, he was put up for interview in front of the nation's media and the questions came thick and fast. Steve replied in his local dialect which, to me, was perfectly understandable.

Not so the assembled football writers. "What did he say?" was their puzzled response. I couldn't see what the problem was but I found myself having to act as interpreter and translate his words from Black Country to the Queen's English.

The Press came to love Bully for his refreshing and approachable manner. My personal affinity with the striker proved invaluable as my journalistic career progressed.

During the 1990 World Cup finals in Italy, Steve was able to help in a way which gave me a helping hand with one of the stories of the tournament.

David Platt's sensational volleyed goal against Belgium in Bologna which took England into the quarterfinals demanded a big follow-up story and an interview with the Aston Villa midfielder.

That was an era long before mobile phones and regulated Press conferences, so John Wragg, of the Daily Express and I went to the England team hotel in search of an interview with Platt, whom we both knew quite well.

Scores of other Pressmen were on the same mission but Wraggy managed to get the number of Platty's room by charming a hotel receptionist.

I was given the task of calling the room. "Hello," said the voice on the other end. I didn't recognise it at first. "Who's that?" I asked. "Who's that asking?" responded the voice. "It's Dave Harrison," I said.

"How do mate," said the voice. "It's Bully. What am yow doin' here?" It turned out Steve and David were room-mates and our Wolves hero invited us up to the room to see the man-of-the-moment who gave us a half hour interview ahead of the rest of the Press pack.

There have been many other occasions when Bully has done favours, notably when it involved charity functions and other goodwill gestures.

Only recently when I was in Rio covering the Olympic Games, I was contacted by a friend who was going to be best man at a wedding of two avid Wolves fans. He wondered whether I could get a message from Steve for the couple on their big day.

I contacted Steve's wife, Kirsty and put the request to her. Within a week she had despatched some video footage of him sending the couple his good wishes in his usual cheerful manner.

That was typical of Bully – generous and affable - but it was only what I have come to expect over the years from one of our own.

Apart from my own kids I must have photographed Steve Bull more than any other person. I have never known anyone who is so easy to photograph. He has such a natural smile and is always prepared to do silly things just to help get a good shot. He normally says 'are you having a laugh?' But then does it anyway. He got so used to me asking him to pose in bizarre situations that eventually he started suggesting his own ideas which were much better than mine.

In the early days the Express & Star sports desk sent me down to Molineux to see if I could get a pic of Bully after he had scored 25 goals for the club. The idea was to get Steve with 25 footballs but the only problem was the club didn't have that many balls in those financially difficult times, so we had go around scrounging whatever balls we could find, including blue, yellow and red plastic ones. But that didn't bother him at all! I hate to think what some Prima Donnas would have said in that situation.

In 1989 I went to a sports shop in Cleveland Street where Steve was signing his first boot deal with Quasar. I didn't know exactly where the shop was positioned but it became pretty obvious when I turned the corner and there were about 500 people queueing outside to get his autograph.

I also remember when Bully and the Wolves team were celebrating winning the fourth division championship and the Wolves midfielder Nigel Vaughan said to Steve: "You won that championship for us," and Bully replied: "Don't be so daft"! I think Vaughan did have a point.

The E&S sent me down to Brighton when Bull made his England debut in the 'B' team alongside Gascoigne, Pallister, Adams and many young internationals. The match was against Italy and I was under pressure to get an early colour image transmitted to the sports desk because the colour pages were pre-printed overnight in those days. Bully didn't let me down.

Ten minutes into the game he went flying past an Italian defender who was at full stretch trying to tackle him. The defender stood no chance and I had my picture! Job done and that was the next day's back page.

The next time I covered Bully playing for England was at Wembley when he scored a brace and guaranteed his place in the Italia 90 World Cup squad. The match was against the Czechs and his first goal was one of the best goals I have ever seen at Wembley.

I was fortunate enough to get a perfect shot of that goal which was used on the Star back page the next day and is now on the wall at Steve's restaurant in Tettenhall.

When Steve was named in the 1990 World Cup squad I was sent with Martin Swain to try and get a story and pic of him at his home in Cheslyn Hay. We didn't know his address so just drove in that direction and when we saw a milkman making his deliveries I asked if he knew where Bully lived. As luck would have it he was Steve's milkman so he directed us to the house and then said: "Don't tell him I told you the address". We knew we had the right address because Bully's sponsored Ford Escort was in the drive with his name blazoned on the side. When he came to the door his first words were: "How did you know where I live?" and I replied: "Because we saw your name on the car." He believed me....I think.

I still work with Bully at Molineux on some matchdays and to be honest it can be a nightmare because every ten seconds he is stopped by a fan for an autograph or a selfie and he just never says no to anyone.

WHAT THE MEDIA SAYS...

CHARLES ROSS

What's in a name?

When it comes to naming a fanzine – quite a lot. It needs to be a little off the wall, humourous, related to its club, easily recognisable. So when A Load Of Bull (or ALOB) began life in 1989, just after Bully had scored more than 100 goals over 2 consecutive seasons – it seemed too good a title to miss.

By standing outside Molineux and countless away grounds selling ALOB, hundreds of times, you do get talking to opposing fans. And the point is this. When they saw that it was ALOB held aloft on sale, they would often make a totally spontaneous, unprompted comment about Steve. Other fans might fear him, but they made plain their respect: for his loyalty, for his effort. They regarded him as a proper footballer, representing what was best about a proper club.

The Black Country symbol is one of an unbreakable chain. Bully had exactly that bond with Wolves fans. It was never all about the money for him. In his Testimonial Year, I was approached by its organisers. He wanted to do something with and for the hard core who had been with him from the start. He wanted to get the fanzine involved, together with Hatherton Wolves (a long established independent supporters' club who ran coaches to away games). The result was a Question & Answer Session with people from ALOB and Hatherton Wolves. It was not held in a swanky function room. Oh no! It was held upstairs in the Varsity pub one wet November night in 1996. A riotous affair! No question was ducked – Steve knew that he was amongst friends. Not one story ever leaked from that room. What did he want by way of donation to his Testimonial Fund? Not a penny. The only thing he asked me for came as we wrapped it up: "Is it alright if I come downstairs for a pint with you lads?" Unsurprisingly – I said "yes". I think that story says a great deal about his values and where his priorities in life lay.

Steve Bull played for the shirt, for the team, for the fans, for the club. He could have gone to Villa, Coventry or others. But no. Instead, he chose to sacrifice his career on the altar of getting Wolves into the Premiership.

The bare statistics tell an incredible story. But it was always about far more than that. It wasn't about the numbers; it was about emotion. By the time those knees finally gave way, he had created a legend and a legacy that has entered the DNA of Wolves. It will survive for as long as the club does.

The lad from Tipton stayed true to his roots, true to the best values of the community from whence he emerged. Hard work, sweat, honesty, loyalty. Whenever he took the field, a part of every Wolves fan took that field with him. He played exactly the way we would dream of playing, if only we had the ability. This, for us, was personal. Deeply so. We kicked every ball with him, we felt every knock he took. Such an emotional bond between fan and player was unique; and it was unbreakable. Loyalty.

What's in a name? In the word "Bully" – quite a lot.

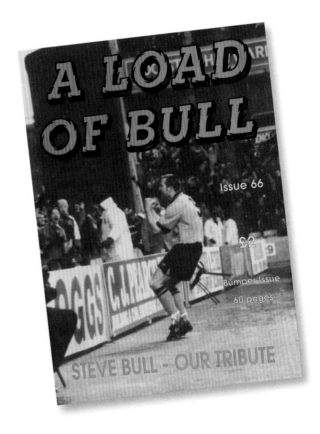

JOHNNY PHILLIPS

I used to love watching Bully score so many goals for Wolves – he almost single-handedly restored so much pride in the club and from the supporters.

In no time at all, from those dark days of November, 1986, he came to represent Wolves and gave an identity back to the town.

That he was a local lad with a remarkably unassuming character made it even more of a special story.

He is one of the few footballers that fans could relate to.

More recently my favourite Bully story came from Chris Waddle, when I was covering a game.

It was an England B trip to Iceland in the summer of 1989 and the manager – Dave Sexton I think – had given them a night out but told them not to go too mad.

Anyway, they'd all gone to this club and when they rolled out at midnight, it was still light, as it is at that time in Iceland.

Apparently Bully panicked, thinking it was morning already and he bundled these locals out of a cab and jumped in with the players to try and get back quickly before someone told him it was the middle of the night.

JACQUI OATLEY

From Bros to Bully, almost overnight.

In the late 1980s, the walls of my bedroom were plastered with pictures of Matt and Luke Goss. I idolised them as a teenage girl growing up in Codsall. Then, one day, I saw a football match on television and a switch flicked in my head. This was the sport for me. A short time later, I turned to the back page of the Express & Star and saw an article about Wolverhampton Wanderers. This was my club and in no time I became completely obsessed with the team in old gold and black. Stevie Bull was the folk hero at the time. Down came Matt and Luke. I rolled off the Blue Tac from the back of their pictures, cut from girlie magazines and transferred it to the back of Steve Bull pictures, cut from the Express & Star, the match day programmes, Match, Shoot and other publications.

When Bully scored, we celebrated on the terrace in the South Bank as though Wolves had scored two goals. He was different: an icon, a local superstar, yet one of us. Those Wolves celebrations when Bully scored had an extra shot of energy and adrenaline. Whatever was going on in your life, however bad a week you'd had, it all disappeared with a swish of his boot or a nod of his head. Such was the power that Stephen George Bull had to make us Wulfrunians happy.

I often wondered what I'd do if I were to meet my hero. I got to find out when I met Bully briefly in the old condemned Waterloo Road stand in the early 90s. He happened to be in the office when I was milling around outside. I barely spoke, simply smiled and asked him to kindly sign my Wolves autograph book which I'd bought in the old Portakabin club shop in the North Bank car park. I was thankfully less overawed when I met him some twenty years later. I'd been asked to host a charity Q&A session with him and former Wolves midfielder, Geoff Thomas, in a church in my home village of Codsall. They say "never meet your heroes" but I had nothing to fear. The aura of Steve Bull will never be tarnished. We shall always remember what that man did for our club and what he meant to our fans, even if his image no longer adorns the walls of my bedroom.

WHAT THE MEDIA SAYS...

BOB HALL

Steve Bull probably wasn't everybody's choice to lead Wolves' attack in 1986. For starters he'd played mostly reserve team football – true, scoring a stack of goals. But there was worse. It was in a blue and white striped shirt. And that was a definite no no.

Think back to Molineux's darkest days. Not a nice thought. Graham Turner's task was Herculian . They could not get any lower but he had implicit faith in the scouts who said 'Take a chance'. Good job he did and how the Old Gold rose from the dead.

Everybody loves a sporting hero and all goalscorers are terrace idols. Not since John Richards had Wolves' fans anything to shout about. And then along came Steve.

The haircuts got shorter, the goals flew in and happy days were here again.

I remember early days communicating with him. A furtive glance and a gruff 'Alright' from him. And early interviews weren't easy. His boots did all the talking he needed. In no time at all the headlines writer's dream name was a star. Not just for club but country. His loyalty- akin to Billy Wright's – was immeasurable. Steve blossomed as Wolves blossomed. They needed each other.

Records were broken in some style. And was there any better tussle on the field than with Leicester City's Steve Walsh. The best goal I witnessed as a reporter was at Newport County. He hit it first time from some considerable distance – around half way as I recall – followed by the trademark wheel away, right arm raised.

As the years progressed so did Steve. He became a good and comfortable talker.... fans and others hung on his every word. I was lucky enough to be asked to compere all his events during his Testimonial Year.

We toured just about every corner of the greater Wolves' fan base.... Tuesday nights in Tipton and Oldbury, Shifnal and beyond. Each one packed as, prompted by me and questions from the floor, Steve and his team mates made the day of fans aged between six and eighty.

The final night in the Civic Hall in Wolverhampton was a sell out long before the event. They sat and stood and cheered – and hundreds more waited outside. That was Bully's pulling power.

One minor complaint. He recorded all his goals as they were shown on ITV where I used to work. Once at his house he put a VHS tape (ask your dad) into the machine to show me the start of the compilation.

Laughing as he did so, there I was with brown hair. Yes brown. Cruel or what.

I had a wry smile to myself as, after his playing days and his hair grew longer, it was silver. Touche Steve.

A top player and a top man. Fond memories.

RICHARD 'DICKY' DODD

Well what can I say about the legendary Steve Bull?

A guy who I have had the pleasure to meet whilst working in radio and a guy who has become a friend. I can remember the very first time I met Steve at a charity function. Straight away I could see he was a down to earth guy, who loves his family and wants to give something back. Steve is very humble about the huge talent that he is, in the world of football.

Over the years we have worked together for many different events and each time we have a laugh with each other and we always talk about Wolves, our beloved football club. We both share a huge passion for Wolverhampton Wanderers and our City. I'm proud to know Steve and privileged to be able to work alongside Bully – one of Wolverhampton's famous sons.

MARTIN SWAIN

My over-riding memory of Steve during my time covering his career for the Express & Star was the 1990 World Cup in Italy. I was fortunate enough to be sent to cover the tournament, and ended up carrying a big sackload of fan mail around for Bully! It made travelling around Italy more of a logistical challenge than it might otherwise have been! I had come up with the idea of getting local fans to send Bully their good wishes for the tournament and that I could pass them on when I got to Italy.

I thought we might get 40 or 50. The Sports Editor said 'you're joking, we'll get hundreds!' Never mind hundreds, we ended up getting thousands! Such was the aura of Steve, at that time especially.

I had two huge kitbags and ended up dragging all these letters and cards around from training camp to training camp, and Bully would take a batch of 30 to 40 away each day. That is my favourite memory of Steve, who was absolutely delightful in the way he handled the press all the way through the years. He set off a little bit shy and awkward as you would expect anyone to be when they just start off but his character and personality just blossomed as time went on.

He went on to become a really great spokesman for Wolves. Throughout his career, and even at the heights of his success, that endearing personality never changed. And I suspect that is part of the ingredients as to why he never moved on to another club.

Steve never really pursued a big move like perhaps the players of today might. I think he took a lot of strength from being amongst those who loved him, and that helped make him the player that he was.

I remember him scoring that amazing goal against Bolton, the shot from distance with his left foot. There were lots of games postponed that day – it was freezing cold – and a lot of the national press came along to Molineux to see what this Third Division wonder was all about. There wasn't a lot going on in the game and then, wallop! And the Bull for England campaign gathered pace after that.

It has been a privilege to have watched Steve's progress through the years and also to have remained in close touch with him since he finished playing and moved on to the next chapter of his life.

He is a top bloke.

Bob Hall

With Dicky Dodd

With Martin Swain

THE WOLVES FAMILY...

When you start talking about the phrase the 'Wolves family', there can be only be one person at the head of the table.

And that is the one and only Sir Jack Hayward.

Sir Jack may have passed away in January, 2015, but he will never be forgotten and his legacy lives on.

Sir Jack loved Bully and Bully loved Sir Jack, and, as Bully recalls, they hit it off immediately.

"When Sir Jack walked in the room he was quiet, within himself, a softly-spoken man, but big and bold at the same time - you knew he was the chairman.

When I first met him I thought he was a very nice bloke. From that first day to the last day we got on. He always thanked me for what I did for the club. I started the football off, he started the ground off, we did it together in that respect.

His funeral showed Wolverhampton and the nation what a gentleman he was and what a giver he was. There were so many people out there to celebrate his life and that shows just what kind of a man he was. Nobody had a bad word to say about him. He'd give anybody anything and he gave so much to charity.

He got a glimpse of the Premier League that I didn't get, when we were there in 2003/04, so he outdid me!

I've got an open invite to the Bahamas and I really hope to be able to go there one day and see his legacy.

Sir Jack used to come into the changing room before a game to wish us all the best, that was it.

He respected all the players and they respected him. We played for him as well as the manager. He came in more like a fan than a chairman, he is gold and black through and through."

The last time Bully saw Sir Jack was at his restaurant in Tettenhall, on one of his final visits back to Wolverhampton before his passing.

Sir Jack enjoyed his meal, to the extent that he sent a thank you card which Bully has kept and cherished, to this day.

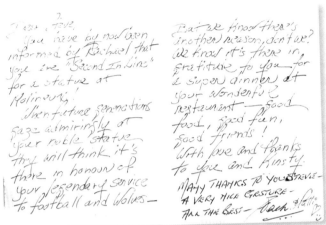

Sir Jack's long-time companion and constant and supportive presence by his side was Patti Bloom, who was herself enthused by the prospect of success for Wolves. And also enthused by the contribution of Stephen George Bull.

We asked Patti to provide her own tribute to mark Bully's 30th 'Wolves' anniversary, both on behalf of herself and Sir Jack.

PATTI BLOOM

Jack Hayward was wildly passionate about two things: his country of birth and Wolverhampton Wanderers Football Club.

It followed that anyone who brought glory to Great Britain or Wolves held a warm, fast place in his heart.

Steve Bull, The Tipton Terrier, with his full-blown Wolverhampton accent, ranked high in Jack's esteem.

One afternoon, as he sat in his flat in Molineux Stadium, Jack picked up the phone and rang Steve Bull. When Steve came on the line, after the usual niceties, Jack said: "Steve, I wonder if you'd approve of my re-naming one of the stands at Molineux after you? I'd like to call it The Steve Bull Stand."

Jack waited out the ensuing silence, imagining that perhaps Steve was overcome with this honour. But Steve eventually replied: "Well, Sir Jack, if it's all the same to you, I'd just as soon have a statue!"

Jack thought for a moment, smiled and then said: "Steve, to have a statue you have to be dead first!" Steve then said, "Oh! Oh, alright, Sir Jack. The stand will do just fine."

Without any doubt, Jack's affection and respect for Steve Bull and his service to Wolves and English football was genuine and lasting. Steve proved Jack's long-held belief that surely Wolves could find the excellence needed in footballing skills from English lads within a fifty-mile radius of Wolverhampton.

Bully was delighted and honoured to become a Wolves' Vice-President and join what was then an illustrious club of three, alongside another couple of Wolves legends in Baroness Rachael Heyhoe-Flint and Robert Plant.

Three recently became four with Ron Flowers also joining the Vice-President ranks and Bully will be looking forward to working alongside Ron for the benefit of Wolves in the future.

He has got to know Rachael and Robert very closely as the trio shared the honour of flying the Wolves flag, also sharing in the joys and disappointments that are synonymous with the famous gold and black!

"At the club Rachael has been like my right arm. When I retired, she took me under her wing on the PR stuff – what to do, what not to do, what to say, what not to say.

She is a lovely lady and will always be in my heart, just like Sir Jack will.

I remember walking onto the pitch with Rachael for Sir Jack's tribute game which was a sad time because we had lost a very good friend. *(pictured right)*

But it was also a celebration.

Nothing is too much trouble for Rachael whether it is for me or for the club and it is a privilege for me to know her.

As for Planty, like Rachael, he is a legend.

He tells me he used to go on tour and with his press badge he had a picture of me on there. Robert Plant with a picture of Steve Bull's face. Can you believe it?

I remember the one game when I think I upset him!

Rob was walking towards the away end with Kevin Rowland from Dexy's Midnight Runners.

I'd had a few beers on the way down there and I saw him and thought 'yes, there's Planty'.

I ran over and jumped on his back and he flung me off and I thought he was going to hit me. I think I'd given him a bit of a shock! But when he realised it was me he said 'alright Bully' and we had a chat and took it on from there.

I think he is like me, Robert. He loves being in there with the fans for games and we both just want to be ourselves and just talk football. He is a great guy and a very generous guy.

When we started the Steve Bull Foundation in 2010, Rob got a band together to play at the launch party. I've got to be honest, Led Zeppelin wasn't really my cup of tea but the music Planty does now I really like. I have been to see him play a number of times. It's toe-tapping stuff and I really enjoy listening to it. I'd recommend it to anyone. He's a good lad isn't he – and what a legend!"

RACHAEL ON BULLY

"Bully has always been a star off the pitch
as well as on it - and yes, I am old enough
to have seen him play for Wolves!

We worked together on many projects when I was
dealing with the Club's work in the Community.

Always willing to support, no matter how off-beat
my requests were, Bully's contribution to the local
community and charity work has been amazing.

We should be proud to have such a
great Ambassador for the club."

PLANTY ON BULLY

"I had never been backstage at a Wolves gig – until
a game we played at Colchester United in 1987.

I knew the owner of the club – my mate
was his driver - and I had taught him several
Wolverhampton Wanderers chants as we drove
from London to Colchester for the game.

By the time kick off arrived I had convinced the owner
that Wolves were made up of a team of world-beaters.

And that was the night that I was left in close
promixity to the marvel that is Steve Bull.

It was after the game, that we won, and Steve
was surrounded by his team-mates. For a rare
time in my life, I felt slightly embarrassed.

I didn't know him and he didn't know me, but I was
so impressed by what he was doing for our club,
along with those other players from his time.

He was a spectacular striker and remains
a great energy around Wolves through all
its changing faces over recent times.

It is good to know him and Bully, if I'm not
mistaken mate, it's my round!"

Being a Wolves Vice-President, as well as a general and constant positive presence around the place, has also led to Bully building up positive working relationships – and indeed friendships – with the Board of Directors.

Directors John Gough and John Bowater enjoyed watching Bully banging in the goals for club and country in his glorious pomp and then, more recently, Jez Moxey and Steve Morgan have tapped into Steve's expertise and experience.

Jez and Steve moved on from Wolves as Chief Executive and Chairman/owner just shy of Bully's 30th anniversary, but they continue to hold him in high affection.

That feeling is mutual.

"I've always got on well with Steve and Jez. Steve is a good man, he has got his own charity and supports a lot of groups in the community.

I remember not long after he had taken over and I took him to a game in Blackpool, along with about 14 others, on a minibus!

He sat on the bus and had a beer or two with us and asked what we thought and when we got back he asked us in for one or two more at Carden Park!

He's a normal bloke, a normal businessman.

He came here and said what he was going to do, put in £30m when he bought the club and he did that. You can't criticise him for what he did and I genuinely think he wanted the best for Wolves.

Steve put his heart and soul into it and we had three years in the Premier League, which we hadn't had for a very long time.

And he carried on the work on the stadium and the training ground which had been started by Sir Jack – the facilities here are amazing now, very different to my time as a player.

Steve wanted the very best for the club and I know Jez did too.

When he came in he was given the job of making the club more financially sound, not losing so much money and over his 16 years he certainly did that.

When other clubs overstretched and ended up in danger of going out of business, Wolves was always well looked after with Jez and he could only ever spend the money that he was given.

I am sure Jez will admit he made mistakes during his time at Wolves and he had the broad shoulders to cope with the fact that he was always the easy one to blame.

But I know how much work he put into his job at Wolves and how much he wanted success and we had a fair bit of it during his time here."

STEVE MORGAN ON BULLY

Much has been written about Bully the legend, the goalscoring phenomenon, incredibly loyal servant to Wolves, etc, but I know him as an all-round top bloke, who is a great mate and always great fun to be with.

From the moment I arrived at Wolves, Steve welcomed me with open arms. From the onset we got on like a house on fire, as we are both 'bloke's blokes', we hold similar values and are passionate about everything we do.

In 2010 we were playing Blackpool away and I joined him and his pals in a minibus to sit in the away end amongst the Wolves fans. A great crack ensued, with a few pub stops on the way. It wasn't our finest hour – we lost 2-1 and a few fans got a bit boisterous at the end, but Steve was there side by side with me to face off the situation. Steve is just one of those guys – if you were ever in trouble you would want him on your side, he is just that kind of man.

I am proud to say that we help each other with our charitable foundations and if I am ever looking for top banter on the golf course, Bully's the man – the only problem is he hits the ball miles further than me!

Sometimes I don't understand Bully's thick Black Country accent, but I do know he's a top man, a great pal and a legend all rolled into one.

JEZ MOXEY ON BULLY

I wasn't lucky enough to be at Wolves to see Steve play in the flesh, as I arrived in 2000, a year after he had retired. But I do count myself fortunate to have had Steve there as a confidante and friend during the 16 years I worked as the club's Chief Executive.

Steve's playing achievements speak for themselves, not only with the goals scored for Wolves and England, but also the incredible loyalty he showed in staying at Molineux when other, more lucrative offers, came calling. He has total love and respect for everything to do with Wolves and plays an important role as a Club Vice-President and as a truly positive and engaging Ambassador and role model.

There have been plenty of ups and downs at Wolves during those last 30 years, but during my time at Molineux Steve always maintained a happy and positive personality, whatever was happening out on the pitch.

I enjoyed our chats about football and about life in general, I enjoyed being alongside Steve at club events and I enjoyed his affable personality and his good humour.

Well done mate - here's to the next 30!

Bully of course isn't the only one to have made Wolverhampton fashionable on a national stage!

Also coming under the recently emerged 'Wolvesaywe' banner are others who have achieved great success and put the city on the map.

In the world of music and theatre there is Beverley Knight and in media and broadcasting, Suzi Perry. The two are also, like Bully, ambassadors of the Promise Dreams charity and have worked with him closely on many charity events.

What do they think of the main man?

SUZI PERRY

Steve was a rare gem on the field. The natural talent was obvious as was the dogged determination to slam the ball into the back of the net, but the loyalty he showed and still shows the club, is unique.

When I first met Steve, many years ago I was alongside my brother. We had watched Bully play many, many times and we thought of him as a local 'demigod!'

Within minutes, we were all laughing and chatting, completely at ease. I'm smiling as I write this because having known him for a long time now, it seems absurd that we were nervous to say hello.

The total commitment he showed to the 'beautiful game' he now shows to a far more important crowd - children in need of help. His work for Promise Dreams is extraordinary. I'm also an ambassador for the Wolverhampton based charity and we work together sometimes to raise money, hosting events etc. He and Kirsty have dedicated their lives to improving those of others. Steve is still a hero on the field, but more of one off it.

BEVERLEY KNIGHT

As a young child, I remember feeling chuffed that Kenny Hibbitt's daughter went to my school. Bragging rights you see.

As I got older, the 'tour de force' that is Bully burst into all our lives. His huge poster took its place among my throng of Prince posters, the only sportsman to do so.

In fact, the only other person full stop.

Can you imagine how I felt as an adult to meet the legend himself, many times over the years?!

Wow, just love him and his uncompromising Tipton dialect.

There have of course been many others of a Wolves persuasion whom Bully has come into contact with over the 30 years.

Among that number proud to have made his acquaintance are two long-serving members of the Wolves staff, club historian Graham Hughes, and programme editor - and fellow historian - John 'Fozzie' Hendley.

With Graham Hughes... *...And Foz*

GRAHAM ON BULLY

I can still remember being around the dressing rooms when Bully and Thommo arrived on the day that they signed. I remember saying a quick hello – and then got to know them well over the years.

I used to make Bully cups of tea and it always had to be sterilised milk. "Mek sure it's 'Sterra' Hughesey," he used to say to me. Despite all of his success he never ever changed. He always stops for a chat and a laugh and a joke.

I was proud to travel up on the train to Manchester to collect the matchball after he scored against Manchester City at Maine Road.

It was the goal which took him past Tony Brown's record in Midlands football, so we wanted the ball for Wolves' archives. Bully was one of those centre forwards who would have been successful in any era.

It was great to know Bully and to watch him score all of those goals. He was helped by a great team and he appreciated how they played a part in all of his achievements. A real Wolves legend.

FOZ ON BULLY...

I have known Bully since he first arrived at Molineux. At the time I helped out in the players' bar when the options were cans of lager, bitter or lemonade. The cans sold at 50p a time and when stocks were running low one of us would be sent to Asda to replenish supplies.

I had a deal with Steve that every time he got a hat-trick I would buy him three cans. He cost me a few bob at the time!

His mom and dad, Joan and George, were regulars. They were Black Country through and through – salt of the earth. I can still picture Joan sat there in her red candlewick coat, handbag on her knees, whilst George gave me an honest assessment of his son's form that day.

Apart from his goalscoring ability, one of Bully's biggest assets is his loyalty. His bond with Wolves proves that but he is fiercely loyal to his friends too. And there is one particular incident that springs to mind involving me.

Wolves were playing a testimonial game and at the end of it I had to do a recorded interview with one of the players. I asked Andy Thompson and he said 'no problem' and to follow him. He led me into the Players/Sponsors Lounge of this particular club and we stood in a corner doing the interview.

I became aware of someone behind me giving me the dirtiest of looks. When I finished talking to Thommo I asked this chap if there was a problem and he snapped back, in the best 'Jobsworth' fashion, "No interviews in here - now get out."

As I passed a table full of Wolves players, Bully asked where I was going. Motioning towards aforementioned Jobsworth I said: "He's chucked me out for doing an interview in here".

"Yow'm with us. Sit down, what do you want to drink?"

Bully stomped off to the bar and returned with the requested pint of lager before telling me to get my tape recorder out. "Right," he said, "now interview us all!"

Jobsworth just glared but it was typical of Bully. Headline grabbing made no difference whatsoever to a bloke who would stick by his mates to the end.

We have seen the tributes from Bully's team-mates from back in the day, but he also remains in close contact with the current crop of Wolves players.

He is at almost all home matches, plus some away and is very much a supporter of the club's current position.

And he is always delighted to see the young players come through and succeed and, if possible, go on and make a name for themselves.

None more so than the current skipper Danny Batth, pictured here chatting to Bully at the Compton Park training ground.

"Danny is a local lad and the fans have taken to him. He always gives 100 per cent and is hopefully here for a good few years to come.

I remember in my day there was Matty Murray, Lee Naylor, Carl Robinson, Robbie Keane and then Joleon Lescott.

Good young players who got a chance at the club and made sure they took it. Danny is another of those – there have been a few over recent years – and I think the fans always love to see the local lads make it and succeed at Wolves."

BATTH ON BULLY

I think any young player coming through the ranks at Wolves knows all about Steve Bull and everything he did for the club.

We may have been too young to see him play but his contribution will never be forgotten – scoring 306 goals for one club is some record!

It is great that he is still connected to Wolves and that we can still bump into him on a matchday or at different events.

He is always happy to chat and offer some encouragement and give his support to the lads.

CHARITYBULL

Always ready to help where he can...

When approached by good friend Suresh Bawa, to help him promote a new charity back in 2001, Bully was only too happy to help.

"Promise Dreams is a charity which makes dreams come true for seriously and terminally ill children. Suresh is the main man there as one of the founders of the charity and is one of my best mates. He approached me and asked me to help launch the charity, which at the time was called Purple Dreams.

I remember it was held outside the Novotel in the town centre and was launched with the release of a lot of purple balloons.

It is all about trying to help children who are in a bad situation, many of whom are terminally ill, with families going through some really tough times.

It is sometimes difficult to meet them, but they are the brave ones and I feel it is important for the charity to try and help the children in some small way.

I am one of the lucky ones who hasn't really had any serious illness in my family, but so many people have and these families are going through such difficult times that Promise Dreams can provide something to try and help them through it.

Even I struggle to see the really poorly children who are just born or really young. I find it too emotional and cannot begin to imagine what their parents are going through. The older children I think I can relate to and talk to and try and help.

We help as many people as we can so it is difficult to single people out. Freya, though, is one girl we have a long association with and it all started with Promise Dreams providing her with the money to build a Wendy House in her garden.

And then there is Neil Taylor, the landlord at the Fox at Shipley, who is another of my good mates.

His daughter Kiahna has had so many operations due to a heart condition and Neil does a phenomenal amount of fundraising for Birmingham Children's Hospital.

Most recently he cycled from John O'Groats to Lands End and then, not long after getting back, flew off to climb Mount Kilimanjaro!

Someone like him inspires me to do more, it really opens your eyes."

And in terms of being inspired, Bully's work with Promise Dreams soon saw him and wife Kirsty deciding to launch their own charity.

It was in 2010 that the Steve Bull Foundation came to fruition, with a launch party headed up by a performance from rock legend and fellow Wolves Vice-President Robert Plant.

"After helping Promise Dreams for a lot of years I started getting a lot of requests from other charities, asking me to help them.

I spoke to Suresh and discussed the idea of me starting the Steve Bull Foundation and splitting the fundraising with Promise Dreams and other local charities who are in need of support.

He was absolutely fine with it and so it went ahead. We have supported a lot of different charities with the Steve Bull Foundation from Compton Hospice to Ronald McDonald House where we sponsored a room.

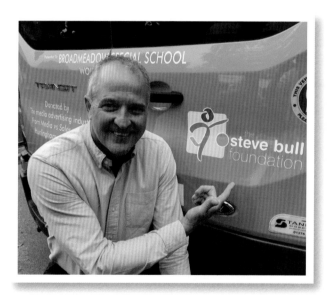

It isn't about me, but it does give you a feeling of satisfaction to be able to help people. It is nothing for me to help and then I go home at the end of the day to my family but will remember that these children and these families continue to face a battle.

It gives you a real sense of perspective and I think anyone who can help a charity in any way should always try and do so."

Bully promoting the Santa Run for Promise Dreams at Tettenhall College (2012)

Mutchy keeps Bully and Steve Walsh apart at the Promise Dreams charity golf day at South Staffs Golf Club (2007)

At the launch of the Steve Bull Foundation with Robert Plant in 2010

At a Steve Bull Foundation Charity evening with Mark Rhodes, Matt Murray, Ben Shephard and Don Goodman

Jody Craddock and Don Goodman join Bully at the Promise Dreams Walk for Dreams at Himley Hall (2014)

Marstons Charity Bike Ride for the Steve Bull Foundation

What lies around the corner for Wolves' Vice-President, record goalscorer and general club legend? One thing's for sure, he is keener than ever to extend that tight-knit association for as many years as possible beyond the current 30.

"I love going to the club and doing what I can, meeting fans and going into the corporate areas.

I still get a buzz when I turn up at Molineux, - it's a very different buzz to playing - but it is still enjoyable.

I can still shut my eyes now and remember turning up when Wolves was a run-down shack and thinking what it is like now. In that sense 30 years has passed so quickly.

I have seen the highs and lows, ups and downs and I wouldn't change anything."

It's a time when change has very much been the order of the day at Bully's beloved Molineux. The takeover of the club by the Chinese-based Fosun Group in the summer, followed by the appointment of Italian playing legend Walter Zenga as Head Coach.

Zenga was the Italian keeper during the 1990 World Cup and was between the sticks for the Azzurri in the third-placed play-off with England, when Bully was an unused substitute. Bully popped to Molineux on the day Fosun's Jeff Shi headed up the media announcement following the takeover and made his introductions. Bully is hopeful there are good times ahead.

"The club is going into a new era now. Fingers crossed they are going to put some money in and they are going to be here for a long time.

It may take a while, it is such a difficult job to get promoted into the Premier League, but it has to be onwards and upwards now.

Maybe Kenny had taken the club as far as he could with the budget he had at the time. He did a great job but I think the team struggled a bit last year and it wasn't as enjoyable going along to games. The atmosphere didn't seem to be there and everyone was waiting for something to happen."

"Now though there is a big buzz about the place after the takeover and there seem to be smiles on faces again – it is exciting. I came in and met Jeff Shi on the day of his press conference to say hello and I think everyone is thinking big again.

Walter Zenga has come in and there seems to be a lot of hard work, passion and spirit in the team, which seems to come from him.

It is enjoyable to go again and I am looking forward to it. I think the owners will want success quickly – they won't be wanting to wait for too long. But through it all I hope they keep the club at heart. Yes football is a business now - and it has to be - but I hope they keep the club at heart in terms of how they run it and the people and the fans. They need to use the expertise of the people already there and then add to it to try and bring success via their investment.

My future? Who knows. I'm still a Vice President. Can they take that off you? I was given a new tie this season so I hope I'm safe for now!

You never know what is around the corner but I love my association with Wolves and it was great to meet Jeff when the takeover went through.

I don't think they will change the structure too much as long as things don't go stale and fingers crossed Wolves are in the Premier League in the next year or two.

We all want to be seeing the Chelseas, the Manchester Uniteds and the Manchester Citys back at Molineux again."

And the future for Bully himself, who turned 50 in 2015?

"I will keep doing what I am doing. I will keep doing charity work, keep trying to get my golf handicap down and keep looking after Kirsty and Gracie.

I don't think there is anything left that I want to do that I haven't done. I've met the Queen, I've been to the Caribbean, I've seen the Pyramids in Egypt – quite a variety! I just want to carry on meeting people and carry on keeping busy if I can.

I've got my family, I've got my friends and I've got my football – I'm not sure I need anything else?"

"FOOTBALL HAS BEEN MY LIFE AND
WOLVES HAS BEEN MY LIFE FOR 30
YEARS. IT STILL IS. IT IS LIKE MY SECOND
HOME. IT'S NOT THE SAME AS PLAYING,
BUT THERE IS STILL A GREAT BUZZ
ABOUT BEING INVOLVED, MEETING THE
FANS AND ABOUT WATCHING WOLVES
PLAY. LONG MAY IT CONTINUE........"